RadioTim AROUND BRITAIN GUIDE

The Heart of England

Researched and edited by
JAMES TINDALL

NETWORK BOOKS

RADIO TIMES AROUND BRITAIN GUIDE
The Heart of England

First published in Great Britain
by Network Books in 1993

Network Books is an imprint of BBC Enterprises Ltd.,
Woodlands, 80 Wood Lane, London W12 0TT

Designed by Paul Simpson
Produced by Lovell Johns Ltd. of Oxford and St. Asaph.

Printed in Great Britain by Victoria Litho, Ltd. London.

A catalogue record for this book is available from the
British Library

ISBN 0-563-36952-3

CONTENTS

Welcome to the **RADIO TIMES AROUND BRITAIN GUIDES**. Each guide covers one specific region of the country.

This new series was conceived to fill two needs.

First, to give the discerning TV viewer and radio listener an effective guide to the major attractions within each region, including a brief insight into why they are worth visiting and information on when they may be visited. This section is sub-divided into a number of different types of attractions including a special listing of attractions that are specifically designed for the whole family.

Second, to provide an overview of the companies responsible for broadcasting within each region and the contribution they make nationally as well as on a regional basis. This section of broadcast information also includes brief guides to some of the most popular programmes generated there, a guide to the major televised sporting venues and a personal view of the region by a local media personality.

The guides are illustrated with a wide range of photographs, most of which were supplied by the individual attractions and I am most grateful for the assistance these establishments and their owners and staff have given us.

The TV stills and other broadcast photographs were provided by the television and radio companies and, again, I am very grateful for the assistance the various press offices have given us during the research on this guide.

As these are the first editions of the **RADIO TIMES AROUND BRITAIN GUIDES** we may well have missed some attractions that you feel should be included. We have travelled each region and trawled all the available information from the local Tourist Information Centres but if you feel that there is something else we should include please write via Network Books and we will evaluate your suggestion with a view to including it in the next edition.

I hope that you find this guide useful and enjoyable.

The Heart of England

A background to ....

The region designated as *The Heart of England* covers some of the loveliest countryside in the whole of Britain and includes the counties of Gloucestershire, Hereford and Worcester, Oxfordshire, Shropshire, Staffordshire, Warwickshire and the West Midlands.

Landscape highlights include the Cotswolds, Malvern Hills, Welsh Marches and some of the most beautiful stretches of the Severn and Wye valleys. These areas offer a great deal of interest for ramblers, naturalists and geologists.

Anne Hathaway's Cottage

The region's historic importance is clearly demonstrated by its major fortifications including **Berkeley, Kenilworth, Studley** and **Warwick** castles. There are also many stately homes including **Blenheim Palace, Charlecote Park, Ragley Hall, Shugborough** and **Warwick Castle**.

Warwick is a rare combination of medieval fortress and magnificent house and is the most visited stately home in the country.

The Heart of England's religious life is shown by its cathedrals, ranging from the historic trio of **Gloucester, Hereford** and **Worcester** to modern **Coventry**.

A rare aerial view of the stronghold and stately home of Warwick Castle

Ragley Hall is a stately Palladian mansion

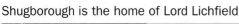

Shugborough is the home of Lord Lichfield

Shakespeare's Birthplace

Holy Trinity Church
Shakespeare's burial ground

In the area of education and the arts the region offers us the colleges of **Oxford Univérsity**, William Morris' **Kelmscott Manor** and William Shakespeare's **Stratford-upon-Avon** as well as a wealth of great museums, the greatest grouping of which is undoubtedly the **Ironbridge Gorge Museums** complex.

Industrial heritage in *The Heart of England* ranges from **Ironbridge** where the world's first iron bridge, built in 1779, still stands to the great pottery and crystal factories of the region including **Coalport**, **Royal Brierley**, **Royal Doulton**, **Royal Grafton**, **Royal Worcester**, **Spode** and **Wedgewood**. There are also some excellent preserved steam railways.

Ironbridge is the home of the world's first bridge constructed of iron

Of the many wildlife reserves in the region the greatest and most famous must be the **Wildfowl and Wetlands Trust** at Slimbridge, the first to be founded by Sir Peter Scott it has a resident population of around 3,300 birds, the largest in Britain.

The region also offers a great range of attractions for days out including model villages, mazes, water parks and zoos. It is also the home of the country's largest and most popular theme park, **Alton Towers**.

"Hot Chefs"

Alton Towers the country's largest and most popular theme park

"A Year in Provence" starring
John Thaw and Lindsay Duncan

"Top Gear" with
Jeremy Clarkson

Television programmes for *The Heart of England* are provided by the BBC's Pebble Mill Studios in Birmingham, ITV's Central TV also from Birmingham and Channel 4, broadcast nationally from London.

The BBC started broadcasting from Birmingham on 15th November 1922 and moved into its well known Pebble Mill building on 10th November 1971. Famous television programmes that have been produced at the studios over the years include **"The Brothers"**, **"Poldark"**, **"Howard's Way"** and **"All Creatures Great and Small"**. The current output includes **"A Year in Provence"**, **"CountryFile"**, **"Gardeners' World"**, **"Hot Chefs"**, **"Kinsey"** and **"Top Gear"**.

BBC's Pebble Mill also contributes more than 2,000 hours of network BBC radio programmes per year including, most famously, **"The Archers"**.

The Wildfowl and Wetlands Trust at Slimbridge

Independent Television reached *The Heart of England* in February 1956, it was originally provided jointly by ATV and ABC and from 1968 onwards by ATV. The company lost a franchise battle during the early 1980s and on 1st January 1982 Central TV took over responsibility for providing programming for the region. Central retained its franchise for a further 10 years from 1993 and is one of the most powerful and profitable ITV companies. Its studio facilities are based at Central House in Birmingham and famous programmes it and its predecessors have contributed to the network over the years include **"Auf Wiedersehen Pet"**, **"Crossroads"**, **"Emergency Ward Ten"**, **"Inspector Morse"**, **"Sunday Night at the London Palladium"** and **"The Power Game"**. The current output includes **"Blockbusters"**, **"Boon"**, **"Just A Gigolo"**, **"Peak Practice"**, **"Sharp"**, **"Spitting Image"** and **"The Cook Report"**.

In addition to its national radio network output Pebble Mill is also the home of BBC Radio WM covering the West Midlands. There is a network of BBC local radio stations covering the region and providing pinpointed local news, information and entertainment.

There are a number of independent radio stations providing commercial local radio for the major cities and towns of the region. The largest of these, BRMB, is again based in Birmingham.

"Spitting Image"

"Blockbusters" hosted by Bob Holness

"Sharpe" with Sean Bean in the title role

"Peak Practice" starring
Simon Shepherd, Kevin Whately
and Amanda Burton

"Inspector Morse"
starring John Thaw
and Kevin Whately

Why I love the Heart of England

Phil Archer

Phil Archer was born on 23rd April 1928 to Dan and Doris Archer. He was 32 years old when the general public first heard about him and he became a national figure within a few months. He fell in love with Grace and married her on 11th April 1955 but, tragically, she was killed in a fire five months later. Happily he found love again, with Jill, and they married in November 1957. The pair, now proud grandparents, moved to Brookfield Farm in 1970 and still farm there.

The actor Norman Painting has played the role of Phil Archer ever since the first experimental episode was broadcast to Midlands radio listeners in May 1950.

So why does Phil Archer love The Heart of England?

Basically it is one of the most misunderstood parts of the country. Unless they live here most people think that The Heart of England is an industrial wasteland of decaying Victorian buildings - it's not!

All right, there are no mountain ranges as such, although the Cotswold Hills, Malvern Hills and Welsh Marches are delightful and offer some stiff hill walks, but the countryside is splendid.

Ambridge and district may be a fictitious creation but similar rural communities are dotted all around this part of the country with village pubs like The Bull, farms that resemble Brookfield and great houses similar to Grey Gables.

As befits an area that has many rural attractions we include amongst them some of the finest gardens in the country including quite a number that were designed by Capability Brown.

To accompany fine gardens there are normally grand houses and castles and Warwick Castle is probably the greatest non-Royal combination of both home and fortress.

Norman Painting
plays Phil Archer in
BBC Radio 4's
"The Archers"

Near to Warwick is Stratford-upon-Avon, it is, of course, world famous because of William Shakespeare and it is undoubtedly because of him that so much of the old town and its surrounding villages are preserved. It is almost impossible to move without seeing something to do with the Bard but at least it means that the area contains some of the best looked after Tudor and Stuart houses in the country.

The River Severn and its many tributaries have a major influence on most of the region and not just for fishermen after trout and salmon!

Again, besides being major landscape features they also exert a significant influence on the rural communities with the water meadows of dairy farms extending to the water's edge.

Of course there are many built up areas within the region, Birmingham being one of the great cities of Britain, but as much as being an industrial focus it is also a commercial and artistic focus with venues that attract world renowned performers.

Basically the heart of England has everything you could want, beautiful countryside, very attractive rural communities, a great number of historic places to wander around and the delights of the big city, if you want them!

TV SCENES
of the Heart of England

A classic Radio Series . . . plus a Great TV Cop
. . . and a TV Soap many regard as a classic

The Heart of England has not been the setting for many great programmes but the three finest of them are some of the most remembered programmes of all time - "The Archers", "Inspector Morse" and "Crossroads".

The Archers

"The Archers" and their friends have been living and farming around the fictitious village of Ambridge for more than 40 years. The first national programme was broadcast on 1st January 1951 although the format had been trialled in May 1950 as a regional programme for the Midlands. It was initially scheduled for a three month run but was an immediate success, attracting audiences of more than 4,000,000 within a year and peaking at around 20,000,000.

Meg Richardson marries Hugh Mortimer

Throughout the years Ambridge has been the setting for many major events and shocks scattered amongst the everyday farming tales. There have been murders and dramatic deaths, none more so than on 22nd September 1955 when **Grace Archer** died in a fire in the stables, coincidentally on the night that ITV first broadcast programmes.

The storylines in **"The Archers"** have always sought to present factual farming information alongside the entertainment of the programmes. This has continued to the present day with experiments in organic farming, debates about EC subsidies and the Archers' use of the Farm Holiday Bureau as an additional source of revenue by taking holidaymakers into **Brookfield Farm**.

The greatest secret of **"The Archers"** success is that the listeners are always led to believe that the characters, farms, **Ambridge** and **Borchester** really exist and are not figments of the scriptwriters' imagination. This feeling is reinforced by touring roadshows by members of **"The Archers"** cast, street plans and maps of the village and even tours of "mock" Ambridge locations.

Crossroads

Angus Lennie as Shughie McFee and Noele Gordon as Meg Richardson in "Crossroads"

"Crossroads" was the programme you either loved or hated. It was mainly hated by the TV critics and many millions of devoted viewers loved it. In fact when it was "killed" in 1988 it was attracting average audiences of around 10,000,000 per episode.

It first appeared in the Midlands on 2nd November 1964 and ran for more than 23 years including, for a period, being broadcast five times a week. It was a story of Midland life focussed on a popular motel run by **Meg Richardson.**

"Crossroads" was not fully networked until 1972 and even then the regions broadcast the programme at different times of the day and were out of synch with one another in the episodes they were showing. In spite of these problems during the early 1970s it was attracting a solid audience of between 6 and 8,000,000.

Meg, played by **Noele Gordon**, was written out of the programme in 1981. Originally the scriptwriters had wanted to kill her in a disastrous fire at the motel but they relented and allowed her to sail to a new life aboard the Queen Elizabeth II.

The wedding of Jill and Adam, Jane Rossington and Tony Adams

Following the fire and **Meg's** departure the motel had a facelift and a series of new owners and managers and even moved up market and was renamed the **King's Oak Hotel**.

The final episode was broadcast on Easter Monday 1988 and attracted more than 13,000,000 to find out whether **Jill Chance** would choose to fight on at Crossroads or go to a new life. Jill was played by **Jane Rossington**, the only member of the cast to last the entire run of 4,510 episodes. She chose the new life and **"Crossroads"** became part of TV history.

Morse's Oxfordshire

Colin Dexter created a unique Oxfordshire Police Inspector who was a deep thinking lover of great music and opera, fine cars and real ales as well as a damn good copper. Zenith Productions worked with Central ITV to dramatise the books using locations around Morse's beloved Oxfordshire and in an inspired piece of casting selected **John Thaw** to play **Inspector Morse**. The first Morse drama was broadcast in 1987 and the rest, as they say, is history.

"Morse" on location in Oxford

By 1992 the first showings of a new **Inspector Morse** series were attracting up to 17,000,000 viewers and reruns of previously shown dramas were attracting up to 10,000,000.

Morse's complex character and diverse range of interests allowed the production team to use many varied locations.

University sites included the interiors of some of the Oxford Colleges, notably Brasenose, as well as the Bodlean Library and the Ashmolean Museum.

Inspector Morse in "The Last Enemy"

Morse's love of music allowed the use of churches and concert halls including the Holywell Music Room, the oldest concert hall in Britain.

His love of real ale, or even something stronger after particularly gruesome discoveries, allowed some of Oxford's finest riverside inns to star as locations for important scenes. One of the most photogenic of these being the world-famous Trout Inn.

Morse's trail around Oxford is so fascinating for lovers of the series that British Heritage Tours organise "Inspector Morse Weekends" so that fans can really soak in the atmosphere!

Worcester
Major televised sporting venues
page 29

Major televised
sporting venues
page 23

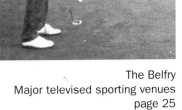

The Belfry
Major televised sporting venues
page 25

MAJOR

TELEVISED

SPORTING

VENUES

in

The Heart

of

England

Athletics

The Heart of England has a number of major athletics venues and the Alexander Stadium in Birmingham has hosted the AAA Championships and the Olympic Qualifiers Trials but the new jewel in the region's athletics crown is undoubtedly the National Indoor Arena.

National Indoor Arena
Central Birmingham, West Midlands
☎ 021 200 2202

The new National Indoor Arena was opened in September 1991 and has already become established as a world-class athletic and sporting facility. In April 1993 it hosted the prestigious opening ceremonies of the World Gymnastics Championships and between now and 1995 it will be the venue for a number of European and World Championships in sports including Badminton, Netball and Table Tennis. The main athletics track is Britain's first demountable six lane 200 metre track and with the track in place the Arena can still hold 8,000 spectators. With the track removed the central area forms a hall 100m by 60m and can seat up to 11,000 for gymnastic events or 13,000 for boxing matches. Major events are often mounted jointly with the Birmingham International Convention Centre and the National Exhibition Centre and the National Indoor Arena is also a major venue for concerts and other leisure events.

The new National Indoor Arena has already become established as a world-class athletic and sporting facility

Cricket

The Heart of England has three County Cricket sides, Gloucestershire, Warwickshire and Worcestershire, and a number of Minor Counties sides but has only one Test Match venue, Edgbaston.

Edgbaston Cricket Ground

Edgbaston, Birmingham, West Midlands
☎ 021 446 4422

Edgbaston is the home ground of Warwickshire County Cricket Club and a Test Match and One - Day International venue. Warwickshire were founded in 1882 and moved to the Edgbaston site in 1886. The ground staged its first Test Match in 1902 when England played Australia and is regarded by many as one of the most attractive Test Match venues. The ground also houses a museum of cricketing memorabilia.

Football

The Heart of England is currently the home of two FA Premier League clubs, Aston Villa and Coventry.

Aston Villa Football Club

Birmingham, West Midlands
☎ 021 327 2299

Aston Villa were founded in 1874, were founder members of the Football League in 1888 and moved into their present Villa Park ground in 1897. Over the course of their long history they have won the League Championship seven times and the FA Cup seven times but the last of either of these was the League Championship in 1981. The Villans also won the European Cup in 1982. Villa Park's current capacity is just over 40,000.

Coventry City Football Club

Coventry, West Midlands
☎ 0203 223535

Coventry City were founded in 1883 although they were called the Singers Football Club until 1898. Coventry City, also known as the Sky Blues, have played at the Highfield Road Stadium since 1899 although the ground was substantially redeveloped with the creation of three new stands in the 1960s and 1970s. It has a current capacity of slightly over 25,000. Coventry City's greatest success to date was winning the FA Cup in 1987.

Golf

Until 1985 *The Heart of England* was never seriously regarded as the home of golf courses of international championship standard, the region possessed many fine courses but none rivalled St. Andrews, Birkdale or Royal St. George's. However, the best professional advisors and golfing architects had been retained to develop a golfing and hotel complex to the north east of Birmingham and, in 1985, Tony Jacklin's Europe team met and beat the USA team at the Belfry. *The Heart of England* now had a piece of golfing legend.

The Belfry

Wishaw, Warwickshire
☎ 0675 470301

The Brabazon Course at the Belfry has been the venue for two Ryder Cups, in 1985 and 1989 and will host its third in September 1993. The Brabazon was always a tough course but additional work on it prior to this year's Ryder Cup has made it even more difficult and it is now an 18-hole 7,182 yard complex of bunker and water hazards with a par of 72. For the less adventurous there is also the Derby Course, build over similar terrain but with easier holes. The Belfry's grounds cover more than 300 acres of parkland and in addition to the two courses there are numerous leisure facilities attached to the complex's 4-star hotel. Visitors are welcome to play both courses although golfers must have a handicap certificate before playing the Brabazon. The courses are very busy and must be booked in advance, the hotel offers golfing breaks and weekends.

Horse racing

The Heart of England is home to eight of the country's racecourses and most are National Hunt courses. They include Cheltenham, the "Home of National Hunt Racing" and venue for the annual National Hunt Festival as well as a number of very attractive country courses. As a general rule all racecourses offer visitors a choice of three different types and prices of daily admission. These three are normally known by the following names although some courses do use other alternatives: Member or Club Enclosure, allowing the visitor to use the entire range of racecourse facilities and services including members-only restaurants and bars; Tattersalls, Grandstand or Paddock Enclosure, providing visitors with their own seating, betting and refreshment facilities and offering access to the Parade Ring; and, Silver Ring or Course Enclosure, offering an opportunity to spend a day at the races for less than £5.

Cheltenham Racecourse

Prestbury Park, near Cheltenham,
Gloucestershire
☎ 0242 513014

Cheltenham deservedly carries the title "The Home of National Hunt Racing", it has a 1 mile 3 furlong left handed oval track and hosts 17 days of national hunt racing per year including the prestigious National Hunt Festival every March. Cheltenham was founded in 1831 although the present course was first used in 1902 and restructured in 1966. It hosts meetings between the end of September and early May each year. The National Hunt Festival is normally attended by around 50,000 racegoers and features the Champion Hurdle and Queen Mother Champion Chase as well as the famous Cheltenham Gold Cup, a 3 mile 2 furlong race for horses aged 5 or over that was first run in 1924. The second most important meeting at Cheltenham happens each November and is centred around the running of the Mackeson Gold Cup. There are many events and attractions on racedays and the racecourse is also the home of the Cheltenham Hall of Fame with displays telling the history of the racecourse and the National Hunt Festival and reliving its greatest moments. The Hall of Fame is open every weekday. Additional stands and enclosures and a range of attractions are available during the National Hunt Festival but because it is so popular it is extremely advisable to reserve day tickets well in advance of the meeting.

Cheltenham

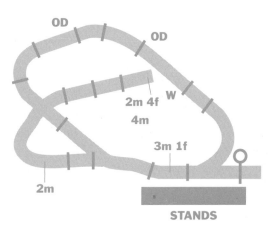

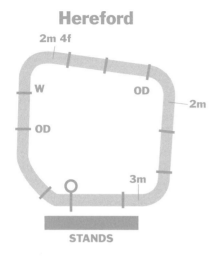

Hereford Racecourse

Hereford, Herefordshire
☎ 0432 273560

Hereford Racecourse was founded in 1842 and hosts National Hunt racing, it has a 1 mile 4 furlong right handed square track. It hosts 15 race days per year and is the only National Hunt racecourse in the country to offer a race meeting on the same day as Aintree's Grand National. Its most popular meetings are on Easter Bank Holiday Monday and Spring Bank Holiday Monday.

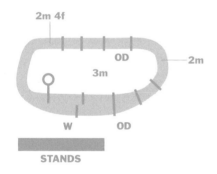

Ludlow Racecourse

Bromfield, near Ludlow, Shropshire
☎ 058477 221

Ludlow is a small rural course in an idyllic part of the country, it was founded in 1868 and hosts National Hunt racing. The course is a 1 mile 4 furlong right handed oval track and there are 12 race days per year. It is a local course and many of its meeting are held mid-week and include races for amateurs.

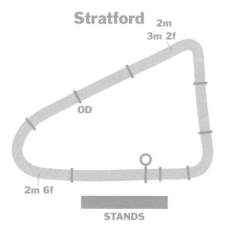

Stratford-on-Avon Racecourse

Stratford-on-Avon, Warwickshire
☎ 0789 267949

The racecourse was founded in 1880 and is the venue for National Hunt meetings. It has a 1 mile 2 furlong left handed triangular track and hosts 14 race days per year between September and June. The most important meeting at Stratford-on-Avon is the two-day Hare and Hounds Meeting held at the end of May/start of June.

Uttoxeter

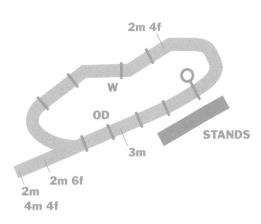

Uttoxeter
Uttoxeter, Staffordshire
☎ 0889 562561

Uttoxeter Racecourse is mainly used for National Hunt racing but also hosts two evening flat racing meetings in June. It has a 1 mile 2 furlong left handed oval track and hosts 21 race days per year. The course was founded in 1907 and its most important race is the Midlands Grand National which it hosts in April. Uttoxeter has been voted the best racecourse in East Anglia and the South Midlands every year for the last three years.

Warwick

Warwick Racecourse
Warwick, Warwickshire
☎ 0926 491553

Warwick hosts both flat racing and National Hunt jumping and has a 1 mile 6 furlong left handed oval track. It has 25 race days per year with racing every month except for September. The racecourse was founded in 1714, many of the present buildings were constructed during the Edwardian era and still display the elegance and spaciousness of the period. Warwick stages a number of important National Hunt events that are used by trainers as trials for both Cheltenham and Aintree. The most important flat race of the year is the Warwick Oaks which is held every June.

Wolverhampton

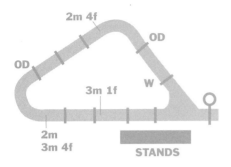

2m 4f

OD

OD

3m 1f

W

2m
3m 4f

STANDS

Worcester

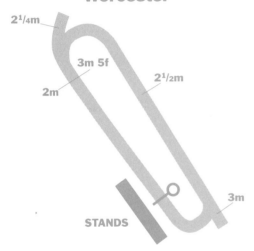

2¼m

3m 5f

2½m

2m

STANDS

3m

Wolverhampton

Wolverhampton, West Midlands
☎ 0902 24481

Wolverhampton hosts both flat racing and National Hunt jumping and has a 1 mile 4 furlong left handed triangular track. There are 26 race days per year with meetings every month including five evening meetings during the Summer.

Worcester

Worcester, Worcestershire
☎ 0905 25364

Worcester Racecourse was founded in 1867 and is a National Hunt venue with a 1 mile 5 furlong left handed oval track. It hosts 20 race days between mid August and mid May.

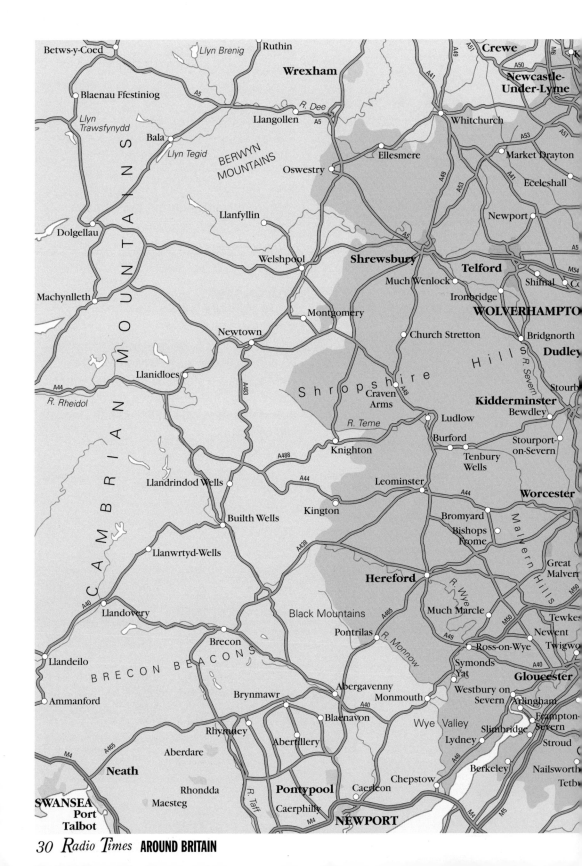

Betws-y-Coed   Llyn Brenig   Ruthin

Wrexham

Blaenau Ffestiniog

A5

R. Dee   Whitchurch

Llyn Trawsfynydd

Llangollen   A5

Bala

Llyn Tegid

BERWYN MOUNTAINS

Oswestry

Ellesmere

Crewe

A50

Newcastle-Under-Lyme

A53

Market Drayton

Eccleshall

Newport

Dolgellau

Llanfyllin

Welshpool

Shrewsbury

Telford

Shifnal

M54

A5

Machynlleth

Montgomery

Much Wenlock

Ironbridge

WOLVERHAMPTO

Newtown

Church Stretton

Bridgnorth

Dudley

C A M B R I A N   M O U N T A I N S

Llanidloes

A44

R. Rheidol

A483

S h r o p s h i r e

Craven Arms

A49

H i l l s

R. Severn

Stourb

Kidderminster

Bewdley

R. Teme

Ludlow

Knighton

A488

Burford

A44

Tenbury Wells

Stourport-on-Severn

Llandrindod Wells

Leominster

A44

Worcester

Kington

Builth Wells

Bromyard

Bishops Frome

A438

Llanwrtyd-Wells

M a l v e r n   H i l l s

Great Malvern

M50

A40

Hereford

R. Wye

Much Marcle

Tewkes

Llandovery

Black Mountains

A465

M50

Newent

Twigwo

Pontrilas

A49

Ross-on-Wye

A40

Llandeilo

B R E C O N   B E A C O N S

Brecon

R. Monnow

Symonds Yat

Gloucester

Ammanford

Brynmawr

Abergavenny

Monmouth

A40

Westbury on Severn

Arlingham

Frampton-Severn

Blaenavon

Wye Valley

Slimbridge

Rhymney

Aberfillery

Lydney

Stroud

Aberdare

A48

Berkeley

Nailsworth

Neath

M4

A465

Chepstow

Tetb

Rhondda

R. Taff

Pontypool

Caerleon

SWANSEA
Port Talbot

Maesteg

Caerphilly

M4

NEWPORT

M4

M5

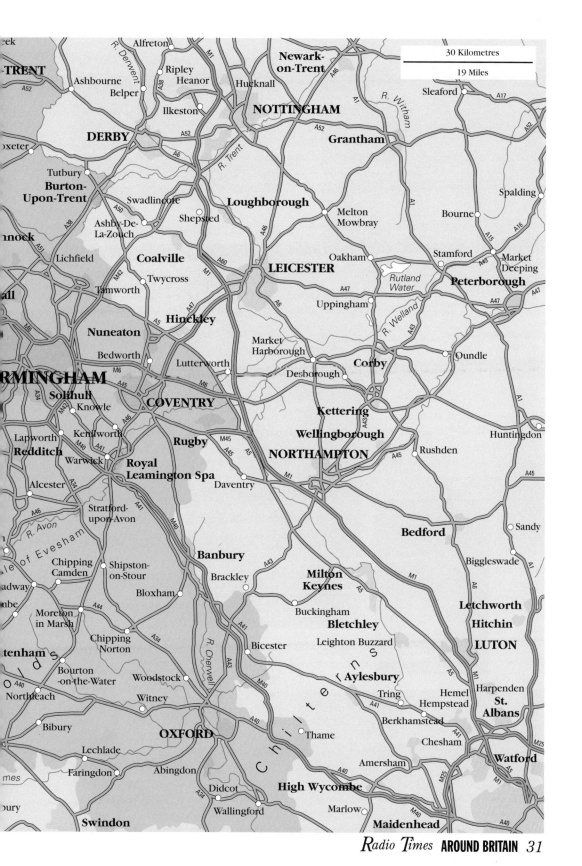

1. Robert Ople Museum
2. Coventry Cathedral
3. Alton Towers
4. Twycross Zoo
5. Burtford House Gardens
6. Jackfield Tile Museum

What to see in

The Heart of England

HOW TO USE THIS SECTION

The attractions are listed under the following categories:

PARKS & GARDENS
ANTIQUITIES
HISTORIC BUILDINGS
RELIGIOUS BUILDINGS
MUSEUMS & ART GALLERIES
WORKING ATTRACTIONS
STEAM RAILWAYS
FOOD & DRINK
WILDLIFE
THE REGION AT PLAY

When an attraction is of interest in more than one category, particularly for example Historic Buildings many of which also have interesting Parks and Gardens, then other entries for the attraction are cross-referenced at the end of the attraction's listing.

For each attraction the following information is provided:

**NAME OF ATTRACTION
NEAREST TOWN OR VILLAGE or
AREA OF CITY**
these are not directional guides and should be used in conjunction with a good road atlas

PARKS & GARDENS

Alton Towers
Alton, near Stoke on Trent, Staffordshire

Britain's largest and most popular theme park. The 200 acres of grounds contain 125 different rides and attractions. Its famous white-knuckle rides include the Corkscrew, the Black Hole, the Grand Canyon Rapids Ride and Thunderlooper, Britain's largest single loop rollercoaster. All types of catering are also available on site.

Open daily from the end of March to early November.

☎ 0538 702200

BRIEF DESCRIPTION OF THE ATTRACTION
with information on its greatest points of interest and notes on shops and refreshment facilities

OPENING PERIODS
when the attraction is open during the year, actual hours of opening should be confirmed by a telephone call to the attraction, please note that even when an attraction describes itself as "Open All Year" it might well close over the Christmas Period

TELEPHONE NUMBER
to enable you to contact the attraction direct in order to check for special events or confirm its suitability for disabled people, large parties, etc. The majority of attractions charge admission and the current prices can be confirmed by telephoning the attraction

PARKS & GARDENS

Abbey Dore Court Gardens

Abbey Dore, near Pontrilas,
Herefordshire

4 acres of gardens including a river garden, rock garden, herb garden, fern garden, walled garden and walled orchard. Plants and gifts are for sale as are light refreshments.

Open late March to late October, closed on Wednesdays.

☎ 0981 240419

Attingham Park

Atcham, near Shrewsbury,
Shropshire

This elegant 18th century house is surrounded by a landscaped estate containing a deer park and woodlands. There is a network of walks through the estate and picnic sites along the Mile Walk. There is also a tea room.

The Park is open every day except Christmas Day, the House is only open at limited period, See "Historic buildings" entry for details.

☎ 074 377 203

SEE ALSO *HISTORIC BUILDINGS*

PARKS & GARDENS

Barnsley House Gardens

Barnsley, near Bibury,
Gloucestershire

Rosemary Verey created these gardens and they feature a rock rose walk, a laburnum walk, a knot garden and 18th century summerhouses containing rare plants, shrubs and trees. There is also a decorative potager of vegetables, fruits and herbs. The gardens also sell selected plants and shrubs.

Open every Monday, Wednesday, Thursday and Saturday

☎ 0285740 281

Batsford Park Arboretum

Batsford, near Moreton-in-the-Marsh,
Gloucestershire

50 acres of gardens containing more than 1,000 species of trees. The layout was influenced by Japanese garden work and features oriental statues, flowering cherries and more than 50 species of magnolia. The Arboretum also contains a picnic area, garden centre, shop and tea shop. Batsford Park also houses a falconry centre.

Open March to mid-November.

☎ 0386 700409

SEE ALSO *WILDLIFE*

Barnsley House Gardens

PARKS & GARDENS

Berkeley Castle
Berkeley, Gloucestershire

840 year old castle surrounded by an ornamental Elizabethan garden and parklands with herds of deer and flocks of wild geese. The garden also contains a Butterfly House with insects in free-flight in a sub-tropical environment. There is a picnic area, tea room and shop.

Summer months only except by appointment.

☎ 0453 810332

SEE ALSO *HISTORIC BUILDINGS*

Biddulph Grange Gardens
Biddulph, Staffordshire

This amazing 15 acre garden was created in Victorian times by James Bateman to display his plant collections from around the world. Acquired by the National Trust in 1988 it has now been restored to its Victorian splendour. The area is divided into a series of small themed gardens including an Egyptian garden, a Chinese garden, an Italian garden and an American garden. The gardens are further enhanced by water features and by buildings designed to reflect the locations of the gardens including a Chinese pagoda, an Egyptian court and a Joss house. There is a tea room and a shop.

Open Wednesdays to Sundays and Bank Holidays between April and the end of October, also open at weekends in November and December.

☎ 0782 517999

Birmingham Botanical Gardens
Edgbaston, Birmingham, West Midlands

The 15 acres of gardens feature a wide and impressive collection of

PARKS & GARDENS

plant species. Temperate and tropical plants are also on display in their own environmentally-controlled glasshouses. The Gardens also house an aviary and have a gift shop, plant centre, play area and restaurant.

Open every day except Christmas Day.

☎ 021 454 1860

Blenheim Palace
Woodstock, Oxfordshire

The stately home of the Duke of Marlborough. The Palace was designed by Vanbrugh and is one of the finest examples of English Baroque architecture. The 2,000 acres of surrounding parkland were landscaped by Capability Brown and make magnificent use of water features. There is a garden centre within the park. Other attractions at Blenheim include the Winston Churchill exhibition, a narrow-gauge railway, a maze, a butterfly house and an adventure playground. There are restaurants, cafeterias, picnic spots and a gift shop.

Open daily from mid March until the end of October.

☎ 0993 811325

SEE ALSO *HISTORIC BUILDINGS AND THE REGION AT PLAY*

PARKS & GARDENS

Burford House Gardens
Burford, near Tenbury Wells, Worcestershire

This is a small garden, only 4 acres in area, but is internationally famous. Its collection of plants has been built up over the last 30 years and includes many rare and unusual species, particularly of clematis. There is also an exhibition of the history of the clematis. The adjoining nursery sells a wide range of the plants that can be seen in the gardens.

The nursery is open every day, please telephone for details of the garden's opening days.

☎ 0584 810777

Buscot Park
Faringdon, Oxfordshire

The gardens used to be one of the most important surviving English formal gardens and were originally created between 1680 and 1730. They were seriously neglected for some years but are now in the process of being expertly restored to their former glory as are the buildings within the gardens.

Open from Easter to the end of October except for Thursdays.

☎ 021 749 4100

Birmingham Botanical Gardens

PARKS & GARDENS

Charlecote Park

Charlecote, near Warwick,
Warwickshire

The Charlecote Park estate is cared
for by the National Trust. The present
house was built in the 1550s and has a
fine Elizabethan gatehouse. The
grounds were landscaped by
Capability Brown and contain herds
of both red and fallow deer, earlier
generations of which were reportedly
poached by William Shakespeare, and
a flock of Jacob sheep. There is a
Music Festival in the grounds in June.
There are picnic spots in the deer
park, a tea room and a shop.

**Open from April to October
except for on Mondays [other
than Bank Holidays] and
Thursdays.**

☎ 0789 470277

SEE ALSO *HISTORIC BUILDINGS*

Croft Castle Estate

Near Leominster, Herefordshire

1,300 acres of open parkland
surrounding Croft Castle. Owned by
the National Trust. The grounds
include an avenue of 350 year old
Spanish Chestnut trees and fine
specimens of mature Oak and Beech.
At its highest point the estate reaches
more than 1,000 feet above sea level,
from this viewpoint you can see over
14 counties with the mountains of
Wales in the background. Iron Age

PARKS & GARDENS

men built Croft Ambrey, a pre-historic
hill fort, on top of this commanding
height and its remains are still clearly
visible.

The Estate is open all year.

☎ No telephone for the Estate, the
Castle's number is 056 885 246.

SEE ALSO *HISTORIC BUILDINGS*

Frampton Court

Frampton-upon-Severn,
Gloucestershire

The gardens of this Georgian stately
home are Grade 1 listed by English
Heritage and include an ornamental
canal. Other features of the garden
are an Orangery and a 17th century
dovecote. The house was built in 1732
for forebearers of the present
occupants.

All year by prior appointment.

☎ 0452 740267

SEE ALSO *HISTORIC BUILDINGS*

Hartshill Hayes Country Park

Near Nuneaton, Warwickshire

136 acres of woodlands and hillside
overlooking the Anker Valley. There
are waymarked paths through the
woods, picnic sites and a children's
adventure playground. The site is

PARKS & GARDENS

reputedly where Queen Boudicca was
defeated by the Romans.

Open all year.

☎ 0827 872660

Hidcote Manor Gardens

Hidcote Bartrim, near Chipping
Camden, Gloucestershire

Modern gardens created by Major
Lawrence Johnston and featuring a
series of small themed gardens
including the white garden, the
fuchsia garden and the stilt garden.
There is also a tea room and shop.

**Closed in winter and on Tuesdays
and Fridays.**

☎ 0386 438333

Hodnet Hall Gardens

Hodnet, near Market Drayton,
Shropshire

The Elizabethan style hall is
surrounded by 60 acres of landscaped
gardens, lakes and woodlands. There
are walks around the Gardens. The
kitchen garden sells its produce and
there is a gift shop and a 17th century
tea room.

Open April to September.

☎ 063 084 202

Lingen Nursery and Garden

Lingen, north west of Leominster,
Herefordshire

The gardens make full use of the
rugged Welsh Marches countryside
to demonstrate rock gardens, peat
gardens, scree gardens and alpine
gardens and the effective use of
herbaceous borders within these
environments. The nursery in the
Gardens sells a wide range of alpine
and herbaceous plants.

Open February to November.

☎ 0544 267720

Burford House Gardens

PARKS & GARDENS

Moseley Hall Fordhouses
near Wolverhampton, West Midlands

The gardens of this 17th century National Trust house have been recreated to show the way they would have appeared when the house had just been built. There is a knot garden, a herb garden and a nut walk. There is a shop and a tea room.

Open on Wednesdays, Weekends and Bank Holidays between April and October, also open on Tuesdays in July and August.

☎ 0902 782808

SEE ALSO HISTORIC BUILDINGS

Oxford University Botanic Gardens
Oxford, Oxfordshire

The oldest botanic gardens in the country, founded by the Earl of Danby in 1621. The collections include outdoor gardens and glasshouses as well as water plants and specialist rock and bog gardens. There are more than 8,000 species in the collections.

Open every day.

☎ 0865 276920

PARKS & GARDENS

Packwood House
Hockley Heath, near Lapworth, Warwickshire

This timber framed Tudor house is a National Trust property. The gardens are much admired, particularly for their Yew trees and the topiary of the trees. It also has a Carolean Garden. There is a picnic site in the gardens.

Open from Wednesday to Sunday and Bank Holidays between April and October.

☎ 0564 782024

SEE ALSO HISTORIC BUILDINGS

Queenswood Country Park
Near Leominster, Herefordshire

An award-winning arboretum featuring more than 500 different species of tree from around the world. The Park also includes a nature reserve, visitor centre, picnic site and waymarked trails.

Open all year

☎ 056884 7052

PARKS & GARDENS

Ragley Hall
Near Alcester, Warwickshire

The stately home of the Earl of Yarmouth is a 17th century Palladian mansion containing what is regarded as the finest Baroque plasterwork in England. The landscaped gardens and park were designed by Capability Brown. There are walks through the woodlands, an adventure area in the woods and a 3-dimensional maze. There are picnic places around the lakeshore and a tea room overlooking the Rose Garden.

Open from Easter to the end of September apart from on Mondays [other than Bank Holidays] and Fridays.

☎ 0789 762090

SEE ALSO HISTORIC BUILDINGS AND THE REGION AT PLAY

Ryton Gardens National Centre for Organic Gardening
Ryton-on-Dunsmore, near Coventry, Warwickshire

Gardens created and cultivated naturally using no pesticides or artificial fertilizers. Within the show gardens you can see trees, shrubs, flowers, fruits, vegetables and herbs all being grown the natural way. The grounds include a lake, play area and picnic site.

Open every day.

☎ 0203 303517

Shugborough Estate
Milford, near Stafford, Staffordshire

The ancestral home of the Earls of Lichfield, Shugborough Hall is an 18th century mansion set in a 900 acre estate. The Hall's formal gardens include Victorian terraces and rose gardens. The surrounding parkland contains eight famous neo-Classical monuments and follies. There are extensive woodland walks through the estate. The estate's Home Farm is

The Oxford University Botanic Gardens are the oldest in the country

PARKS & GARDENS

being used as a working 19th century farm with rare breeds and a restored corn mill. There is a special area of the farm devoted to introducing children to farm animals. The estate also includes the Staffordshire County Museum. There are tea rooms, a shop and picnic areas.

Open every day between the end of March and the end of October.

☎ 0889 881388

SEE ALSO *HISTORIC BUILDINGS AND WORKING ATTRACTIONS*

Studley Castle Gardens
Winchcombe, Gloucestershire

Studley Castle is a magnificent Tudor castle surrounded by splendid formal Elizabethan gardens. The centrepiece is the Queen's Garden, named after Kathcrine Parr who is buried in the castle's chapel. It is a parterre planted with roses, edged by herbs and flanked by 15 feet tall double yew hedges. There is also a knot garden and topiary and the tithe barn contains a collection of old English roses. The castle hosts many craft events and there is an adventure playground and a restaurant.

Open from April to October.

☎ 0242 602308

SEE ALSO *HISTORIC BUILDINGS AND THE REGION AT PLAY*

PARKS & GARDENS

Trentham Gardens
Trentham, Stoke on Trent, Staffordshire

800 acres of landscaped gardens, parkland and a lake. The gardens also have a nature reserve, crafts centre and extensive leisure and sporting facilities. There is a restaurant and a cafe.

Open every day between Easter and October.

☎ 0782 657341

SEE ALSO *THE REGION AT PLAY*

Warwick Castle
Warwick, Warwickshire

Warwick Castle is surrounded by 60 acres of grounds. The gardens around the castle include a Peacock Garden, Rose Gardens and a Conservatory. The rest of the grounds include woodlands and feature nature trails, riverside walks and woodland walks. The present medieval fortress was created by the Beauchamp family in the 14th century. Over the centuries the castle has served as both a military stronghold and great baronial stately home and both the fortifications and State Rooms at Warwick are worth inspection. Many of the castle's rooms contain exhibitions and

Trentham Gardens has 800 acres of gardens and parks

PARKS & GARDENS

displays including medieval armour and reconstructions by Madame Tussaud's. There is a restaurant, catering and picnic areas. Warwick Castle is the most visited stately home in Britain.

Open every day except Christmas Day.

☎ 0926 495421

SEE ALSO *HISTORIC BUILDINGS AND THE REGION AT PLAY*

Westbury Court Gardens
Westbury-on-Severn, near Gloucester, Gloucestershire

This formal Dutch water garden is owned by the National Trust. The network of gardens divided by canals and yew hedges was laid out between 1696 and 1705 and is the earliest known garden of its kind remaining in England. It was derelict until 1966 but has now been lovingly restored.

Open on Bank Holidays and Wednesdays to Sundays between April and October.

☎ 0452 760461

Westonbirt Arboretum
Near Tetbury, Gloucestershire

Westonbirt was founded in 1829 by Robert Holford and has been owned and managed by the Forestry Commission since 1956. There are more than 14,000 trees and shrubs in its 600 acres and the collection is the greatest in Britain and one of the finest temperate arboretums in the world. Contained within its area are 17 miles of paths and tracks for visitors to wander along.

Open every day.

☎ 0666 880220

PARKS & GARDENS

Weston Park
Near Shifnal, Shropshire

The parklands were designed by Capability Brown and include a deer park containing a herd of fallow deer and flocks of rare breeds of sheep and woodlands with walks. Attractions in the grounds include a miniature railway, tropical house and an adventure playground. Special events are held in the grounds throughout the Summer. The house was built in early Restoration style in 1671. It contains impressive collections of furniture and tapestries and is particularly famous for its collection of fine art. There is a bar, a tea room and picnic areas.

Open daily in August, every day except Mondays and Fridays in June and July and all weekends and Bank Holidays between Easter and the end of September.

☎ 095 276 207

SEE ALSO *HISTORIC BUILDINGS AND THE REGION AT PLAY*

Weston Park was designed by Capability Brown

ANTIQUITIES

Chedworth Roman Villa
Chedworth, near Cheltenham, Gloucestershire

The National Trust own and manage these remains of one of the best preserved Roman villas in England. There is a visitor centre and museum and a shop.

Open Tuesdays to Sundays between March and October and also Bank Holidays, opening more restricted in the Winter.

☎ 024289 256

Lunt Roman Fort
Baginton, near Coventry, West Midlands

The Romans built Lunt around 60AD, probably as one of the results of Boudicca's rebellion. It may have started life as a legion headquarters but the Romans mainly used it as a centre for breaking horses. The site has been uncovered and partly reconstructed. The Granary houses an interpretive centre for the site and a museum of the Roman army.

Daily between June and September except Monday and Thursday.

☎ 0203 832381

Wroxeter Roman City
Wroxeter, near Shrewsbury, Shropshire

The remains of Viroconium are preserved by English Heritage. Built around 150AD it was the fourth largest city in Roman Britain and the present day remains are impressive. There is also a museum displaying finds from the site and a gift shop.

Open daily between April and the end of September, open Tuesday to Sunday every week for the rest of the year except over Christmas.

☎ No telephone number.

HISTORIC BUILDINGS

Ancient High House
Stafford, Staffordshire

Built in 1595 this is the largest timber-framed town house in England. The interior contains exhibitions of furniture, paintings and costumes and also functions as a tourist information centre and heritage shop.

Open Mondays to Saturdays all year.

☎ 0785 40204

Anne Hathaway's Cottage
Shottery, near Stratford-upon-Avon, Warwickshire

A thatched farmhouse set in an English garden. It was the home of the Hathaway family and is furnished with period furniture and memorabilia from the family.

Open all year except for 24, 25, and 26th December and the mornings of Good Friday and New Years Day.

☎ 0789 292100

Arbury Hall
Near Nuneaton, Warwickshire

The Hall has Elizabethan origins but was extensively altered between 1750 and 1800 by Sir Roger Newdegate. It

HISTORIC BUILDINGS

is a rare and fine example of Gothic Revival Architecture. The plaster ceilings are particularly good. The stable block in the grounds has a doorway designed by Sir Christopher Wren.

Open Sundays and Bank Holiday Mondays between Easter and the end of September.

☎ 0827 872660

Ashleworth Tithe Barn
Ashleworth, near Gloucester, Gloucestershire

A 15th century stone tithe barn owned by the National Trust. Particularly noted for its roof timbers and porches.

Summer months only.

☎ No telephone.

Aston Hall
Aston, Birmingham, West Midlands

A Jacobean house built around 1620. The Hall has a particularly fine Long Gallery and its plasterwork is impressive.

Open daily from the end of March until the end of October.

☎ 021 327 2333

Anne Hathaway's Cottage

HISTORIC BUILDINGS

Attingham Park
Atcham, near Shrewsbury, Shropshire

This elegant 18th century neo-Classical house contains magnificent State Rooms holding collections of Italian furniture and Regency silver. The Picture Gallery's collection is also impressive. The house is surrounded by a landscaped estate containing a deer park and woodlands. There is a tea room and shop and picnic sites in the Park.

The house is open in the afternoons from Saturday to Wednesday between mid April and early September, it is also open in the mornings on Bank Holidays during this period, the Park is open every day except Christmas Day.

☎ 074 377 203

SEE ALSO PARKS AND GARDENS

Baddesley Clinton
Near Knowle, Warwickshire

This medieval moated manor house is owned by the National Trust. It was built in the 14th century and has altered very little since 1634. Features of the house includes a chapel, priest holes and family portraits. The

HISTORIC BUILDINGS

gardens include ponds and a lakeside walk. There is a tea room and a shop.

Open March to October from Wednesday to Sunday and Bank Holiday Mondays.

☎ 0564 783294

Berkeley Castle
Berkeley, Gloucestershire

Originally built in 1153 for Lord Maurice Berkeley the castle has been occupied by the Berkeley family for 840 years. King Edward II was murdered here in 1327. The castle was attacked and damaged by Cromwell during the Civil War. Berkeley's treasures include its State Apartments and Great Hall, which was built in 1340. Other interesting things to see include King Edward's Cell in the dungeons and the medieval kitchens and cellars. The gardens contain a sub-tropical butterfly house and herds of deer, there is also a picnic area, tea room and shop.

Summer months only except by appointment.

☎ 0453 810332

SEE ALSO PARKS AND GARDENS

HISTORIC BUILDINGS

Berrington Hall
Near Leominster, Herefordshire

A late 18th century neo-Classical house built for Thomas Harley by Henry Holland. A National Trust property with exceptional decorated ceilings and a maritime paintings collection featuring Admiral Rodney's sea battles. The Hall's grounds were laid out by Capability Brown. There is a restaurant and a regular programme of Summer concerts.

Open at weekends from April to October and Wednesdays to Sundays between May and September.

☎ 0568 615721

Blenheim Palace
Woodstock, Oxfordshire

The stately home of the Duke of Marlborough. The Palace was designed by Vanbrugh and is one of the finest examples of English Baroque architecture. The State Rooms contain displays of fine furniture, paintings, tapestries and sculpture. The Long Library which is 183 feet long and contains more than 10,000 books is particularly impressive. The 2,000 acres of surrounding parkland were landscaped by Capability Brown and make magnificent use of water features. There is a garden centre within the park. Other attractions at Blenheim include the Winston Churchill exhibition, a narrow-gauge railway, a maze, a butterfly house and an adventure playground. There are restaurants, cafeterias, picnic spots and a gift shop.

Open daily from mid March until the end of October.

☎ 0993 811325

SEE ALSO PARKS AND GARDENS AND THE REGION AT PLAY

Berkeley Castle has been a family home since the 12th century

HISTORIC BUILDINGS

Bodlean Library
Oxford, Oxfordshire

The Bodlean is one of the world's great libraries and the oldest in Britain. It was founded in 1602 with a bequest from Sir Thomas Bodley of 2,000 books and now houses more than 4,000,000.

Please telephone for opening information.

☎ 0865 277000

Broughton Castle
Near Banbury, Oxfordshire

This moated castle was founded in the 14th century and greatly enlarged during the last half of the 16th century. It was an important centre during the Civil War as the owners were prominent Parliamentarians. The castle contains impressive plasterwork, panelling and fireplaces.

Open on Wednesdays and Sundays from mid May to mid September and Thursdays and Bank Holidays in July and August.

☎ 0295 262624

Burton Court
Eardisland, near Leominster, Hereford

Most of the present building is Georgian although there is a 14th century timber-roofed Great Hall. Sir Clough Williams-Ellis redesigned the front of the house in 1912. Exhibitions in the house include European and Oriental costumes, ship models and a working model fairground.

Limited Summer opening only, mainly Wednesdays, Thursdays, Saturdays and Sundays, telephone for details.

☎ 05447 231

HISTORIC BUILDINGS

Buscot Park
Faringdon, Oxfordshire

This Adam style house is a National Trust property and was built in 1780. It contains the Faringdon Collection of paintings and furniture. The grounds include a Harold Peto water garden and a walled garden. There is a tea room.

Open between April and September on Wednesdays, Thursdays and Fridays and the second and fourth weekends of each month.

☎ 0367 240786

Charlecote Park
Charlecote, near Warwick, Warwickshire

The Charlecote Park estate is cared for by the National Trust. Charlecote Park has been the home of the Lucy family since 1247. The present house was built in the 1550s although it was extensively altered in the 1830s, it has a fine Elizabethan gatehouse. The grounds were landscaped by Capability Brown and contain herds of both red and fallow deer, earlier generations of which were reportedly poached by William Shakespeare, and a flock of Jacob sheep. There is a Music Festival and a Craft fayre in the grounds in June. There are picnic spots in the deer park, a tea room and a shop.

Open from April to October except for on Mondays [other than Bank Holidays] and Thursdays.

☎ 0789 470277

SEE ALSO *PARKS AND GARDENS*

Chester House
Knowle, Warwickshire

A fine small Elizabethan town house that has been restored and is now used as a public library. The roof beams and brick fireplace are

HISTORIC BUILDINGS

particularly interesting. There is a small formal Knot Garden to the rear of the house.

Open daily apart from Wednesdays, Sundays and Public Holidays.

☎ 0564 775840

Coughton Court
Near Alcester, Warwickshire

This National Trust property dates mainly from the Elizabethan period and has a particularly fine central gatehouse that was built in 1530. It used to be moated but this has been filled. The house was attacked by both sides during the Civil War. Its contents include notable collections of furniture and porcelain. The grounds include a formal garden and lake.

Open at weekends from April to October and daily except Monday and Friday from May to September.

☎ 0789 762435

Croft Castle
Near Leominster, Herefordshire

A National Trust property owned by the Croft family from the time of the Domesday Book onwards. The present building has original 14th century walls and towers although a great deal of the inside was remodelled in Gothic style in the 18th century. The grounds include an avenue of 350 year old Spanish Chestnut trees and lead on to an extensive parkland estate containing Iron Age remains.

The castle is open at weekends between April and October and from Wednesdays to Sundays between May and September.

☎ 056 885 246

SEE ALSO *PARKS AND GARDENS*

HISTORIC BUILDINGS

Frampton Court
Frampton-upon-Severn, Gloucestershire

This Georgian stately home was built in 1732 and is still lived in by the original owners. The house contains a collection of 18th century furniture, porcelain and paintings. The grounds feature an Orangery, a 17th century dovecote and Grade 1 listed gardens.

All year by prior appointment.

☎ 0452 740267

SEE ALSO *PARKS AND GARDENS*

Goodrich Castle
Goodrich, near Ross-on-Wye, Hereford

Ruins of a 13th and 14th century castle built of sandstone on a bluff overlooking the River Wye. An English Heritage property, the castle was partially destroyed by Cromwell during the Civil War.

Open Tuesdays to Sundays between the end of September and the end of March and every day for the rest of the year, closed over Christmas.

☎ No telephone.

Hagley Hall
Hagley, near Stourbridge, Worcestershire

The last Palladian mansion to be built in Britain, constructed in 1760. The Italian plasterwork is particularly impressive. The Hall houses the 18th century Lyttelton Collection of paintings and furniture.

Please telephone for opening information.

☎ 0562 882408

Hall's Croft
Stratford-upon-Avon, Warwickshire

A Tudor town house that was owned

HISTORIC BUILDINGS

by William Shakespeare's daughter and her doctor husband. The house is furnished in period style and one room is equipped to show how a 17th century doctor's dispensary would have appeared.

Open every day except 24th, 25th and 26th December and the mornings of Good Friday and New Years Day.

☎ 0789 292107

Hanbury Hall
Hanbury, near Droitwich Spa, Worcestershire

The Hall is a National Trust property. It was built in 1701 in the William & Mary style using red bricks. It is a typical English country house and has been little altered since the start of the 18th century. The magnificent painted ceilings are by Thornhill. The Hall houses the Watney Collection of porcelain. The grounds include an Orangery and an Ice House. There is a tea room, a shop and a picnic area.

Open Saturdays, Sunday and Monday afternoons between April and the end of October.

☎ 0527 821214

Hanch Hall
Lichfield, Staffordshire

The mansion represents a large number of architectural styles reflecting different periods of extension and renovation. Originally built in the 13th century it contains fine examples of Tudor, Jacobean, Queen Anne and Georgian work. The plasterwork, panelling and staircases are particularly noteworthy. In addition to the principal rooms of the house there is also public access to the mansion's Elizabethan cellars. The house also contains an award-winning 40 feet tall model of Lichfield Cathedral.

Open on Sundays and Bank Holidays from the end of March to the end of September, on Thursdays from early June to

HISTORIC BUILDINGS

September and on Saturdays in July and August.

☎ 0543 490308

Hellens
Much Marcle, Herefordshire

The present mansion at Hellens was built in 1292 by Yseult Lady Audley and is still lived in by her family. It contains fine collections of furniture, tapestries, paintings and other items that the family has accumulated over the centuries. Tudor Queen Mary slept at Hellens and Edward the Black Prince ate there, at a table that is still preserved.

Open Wednesday and Saturdays between Easter and September.

☎ 053 184 668

Kelmscott Manor
Near Faringdon, Oxfordshire

An Elizabethan manor house set in a riverside garden. Kelmscott was the home of the great designer William Morris from 1871 until his death in 1896. Many works of Morris and his fellow Pre-Raphaelites are on display including wall papers, tapestries and carpets.

Open all year.

☎ 0367 52486

Kenilworth Castle
Kenilworth, Warwickshire

Kenilworth was one of the greatest and most important castles in England from its foundation in the early 12th century until it was ruined in the Civil War. English Heritage look after the remains and run a gift shop.
Open every day between April and the end of September and from Tuesday to Sunday for the rest of the year except over Christmas and New Year when Kenilworth is closed.

☎ No telephone number.

HISTORIC BUILDINGS

Little Malvern Court
Malvern, Worcestershire

Built around 1480 as the Prior's Hall for the Benedictine Monastery. The roof is particularly impressive, it is a 5 bay double-collared oak-framed roof. The Court has other evidence of its monastic orgins including Monks' Cells. There is a collection of religious garments and paintings inside the building.

Open daily between mid April and mid July.

☎ 0684 892988

Lord Leycester Hospital
Warwick, Warwickshire

A magnificent group of 15th century buildings. They were first converted for use as a home for old soldiers in 1571 and are still used as such today. The Great Hall and Chapel are particularly interesting.
Open Monday to Saturday all year.

☎ 0926 491422

Lord Leycester Hospital

HISTORIC BUILDINGS

Lower Brockhampton
Brockhampton, near Bromyard, Hereford

A half-timbered moated manor house originally built in the late 1300s, now owned by the National Trust. Only the Medieval Hall and Parlour of the house are open to the public but the grounds also include the ruins of a 12th century chapel and an unusual half-timbered detached 15th century gatehouse.

Open Wednesday to Sunday between April and October and Bank Holidays during the Summer.

☎ 0885 488099

Mary Arden's House and Shakespeare Countryside Museum
Wilmcote, near Stratford-upon-Avon, Warwickshire

The Tudor farmhouse home of Mary Arden, William Shakespeare's mother, and the adjoining Glebe Farm provide the home for a museum of country life.

Open all year except for 24th, 25th and 26th December and the mornings of Good Friday and New Years Day.

☎ 0789 293455

Moseley Hall
Fordhouses, near Wolverhampton, West Midlands

This 17th century National Trust house has fine oak panelling. Some of the rooms include secret hiding places, one of which was used by Charles I when he hid here after being defeated at the battle of Worcester. The bed he used is also still in the Hall. The small formal gardens have been recreated to show they way they would have appeared when the house had just been built. There is a shop and a tea room.

HISTORIC BUILDINGS

Open on Wednesdays, Weekends and Bank Holidays between April and October, also open on Tuesdays in July and August.

☎ 0902 782808

SEE ALSO *PARKS AND GARDENS*

New Place and Nash's House
Stratford-upon-Avon, Warwickshire

New Place is the site of William Shakespeare's last house and the foundations of the house are preserved in the Elizabethan garden. Nash's House, alongside New Place, was the home of Shakespeare's grand-daughter and is furnished in period style. Part of the house also serves as a museum showing the history of Stratford-upon-Avon.

Open all year except 24th, 25th and 26th December and the mornings of Good Friday and New Years Day.

☎ 0789 292325

Packwood House
Hockley Heath, near Lapworth, Warwickshire

This timber framed Tudor house is a National Trust property. Although the Tudor origins are evident the house was altered and added to in the 17th century. The collections inside the house include furniture and particularly fine tapestries. The gardens are much admired for their Yew topiary and Carolean Garden. There is a shop at the house and a picnic site in the gardens.

Open from Wednesday to Sunday and Bank Holidays between April and October.

☎ 0564 782024

SEE ALSO *PARKS AND GARDENS*

HISTORIC BUILDINGS

Pittville Pump Room
Cheltenham, Gloucestershire

The Regency pump room of one a Cheltenham's original spas, Pittville Spa, was opened in 1830. It was built for Joseph Pitt as the centrepiece of his new town development. It is surrounded by Pittville Park and contains a museum of Cheltenham life over the centuries.
Closed in December and January, closed on Mondays except for Bank Holidays and Sundays in the winter.

☎ 0242 512740

Ragley Hall
Near Alcester, Warwickshire

The stately home of the Earl of Yarmouth is a Palladian mansion designed by Robert Hooke in 1680, it has been occupied by the Seymour family for over 300 years. Its interior is splendid and James Gibbs' Great Hall, dating from 1750, is regarded as having the finest Baroque plasterwork in England. The South Staircase Hall houses a new masterpiece, a mural called The Temptation painted by Graham Rust

Ragley Hall is a stately Palladian mansion

HISTORIC BUILDINGS

between 1969 and 1983. The landscaped gardens and park were designed by Capability Brown. There are picnic places around the lakeshore and a tea room overlooking the Rose Garden.

Open from Easter to the end of September apart from on Mondays [other than Bank Holidays] and Fridays.

☎ 0789 762090

SEE ALSO *PARKS AND GARDENS* AND *THE REGION AT PLAY*

Shakespeare's Birthplace
Stratford-upon-Avon, Warwickshire

The house where William Shakespeare was born is a distinctive half-timbered building with many Tudor features. It contains manuscripts, books and other memorabilia of England's greatest playwright.

Closed on 24th, 25th and 26th December and the mornings of Good Friday and New Years Day.

☎ 0789 204016

HISTORIC BUILDINGS

Sheldonian Theatre
Oxford, Oxfordshire

The Sheldonian was built in 1663 and is one of the earliest major works of Sir Christopher Wren. It is used for Oxford university's formal presentations and ceremonies.

Please telephone for opening information.

☎ 0865 277299

Shakespeare's Birthplace

Shrewsbury Castle
Shrewsbury, Shropshire

The castle has an unusual story. It was originally built by the Normans. During the Civil War Cromwell ordered it to be dismantled and it was. It remained in this state for centuries until Thomas Telford, the great Victorian engineer, re-built it. Its rooms hold the museums of three famous Shropshire army regiments.

Open Monday to Saturday all year and on Sundays between Easter and September.

☎ 0743 358516

HISTORIC BUILDINGS

Shugborough
Milford, near Stafford, Staffordshire

The ancestral home of the Earls of Lichfield Shugborough Hall is an 18th century mansion set in a 900 acre estate. The mansion contains collections of English and French china, silver, paintings and furniture. The Hall's formal gardens include Victorian terraces and rose gardens. The surrounding parkland contains eight famous neo-Classical monuments and follies. The estate is being used as a working 19th century farm with rare breeds and a restored corn mill. There is a special area of the farm devoted to introducing children to farm animals. The estate also includes the Staffordshire County Museum. There are tea rooms, a shop and picnic areas.

Open every day between the end of March and the End of October.

☎ 0889 881388

SEE ALSO *PARKS AND GARDENS AND WORKING ATTRACTIONS*

Shugborough is the home of Lord Lichfield

HISTORIC BUILDINGS

Snowshill Manor
Snowshill, near Broadway, Gloucestershire

A National Trust property that was once the home of Henry VIII's wife Katherine Parr. Built in Tudor times it was given a new facade in the 17th century. It houses specialist collections of musical instruments, clocks, toys and Japanese armour. The house is surrounded by formal terrace gardens.

Open Wednesday to Sunday and Bank Holidays during the Summer, opening more restricted in the Winter.

☎ 0386 852410

Stafford Castle
Near Stafford, Staffordshire

The impressive remains of an early Norman earth and timber fortress built on a hill overlooking Stafford. An illustrated trail leads around the Inner Bailey and Outer Bailey and to the recently discovered remains of a medieval borough. There is a visitor centre.

Closed on Mondays except Bank Holidays.

☎ No telephone number.

HISTORIC BUILDINGS

Stokesay Castle
Craven Arms, Shropshire

A very rare example of an English 13th century fortified manor house. One of the manor house's more recent additions is a fine Elizabethan gatehouse. Light refreshments are available in the courtyard.

Open every day except Tuesdays from March to October, also open at weekends only in November.

☎ 0588 672544

Studley Castle
Winchcombe, Gloucestershire

A magnificent Tudor castle containing art treasures and the tomb of Katherine Parr, one of Henry VIII's wives. The castle is set in splendid Elizabethan gardens and hosts many craft events. There is an adventure playground and a restaurant.

Open from April to October.

☎ 0242 602308

SEE ALSO *PARKS AND GARDENS AND THE REGION AT PLAY*

Tamworth Castle
Tamworth, Staffordshire

Tamworth Castle was first constructed by the Normans, it remained occupied for almost 800 years and the extensions and rebuilding over these centuries offer an opportunity to examine military architecture from Norman to Victorian times. The Tudor Great Hall and Chapel and the Jacobean State Apartments are particularly fine. Exhibitions inside the castle include one of the coins minted at Tamworth's famous Saxon mint.

Open every day.

☎ 0827 63563

HISTORIC BUILDINGS

Tutbury Castle
Tutbury, Staffordshire

The picturesque ruins of a 15th century fortress. Mary Queen of Scots was imprisoned at Tutbury. There is a tea room and a shop and there are country walks around the castle.

Open every day between Easter and the end of September.

☎ 0283 812129

Upton House
Edgehill, near Banbury, Oxfordshire

A fine house dating from the 1690s and built from a mellow local stone. The real glory of Upton is in its collections. Assembled by the 2nd Lord Bearsted during the 20th century they include Old Masters, Brussels tapestries, Sevres porcelain and Chelsea figures. The gardens include terraces, lakes and water gardens.

Open at weekends and Bank Holidays from April to October and Saturdays to Wednesdays from May to September.

☎ 0295 87 266

Warwick Castle
Warwick, Warwickshire

William the Conqueror built a castle at Warwick on the bluff overlooking the River Avon to replace a Saxon fort built in 913. The present medieval fortress was created by the Beauchamp family in the 14th century. Over the centuries the castle has served as both a military stronghold and great baronial stately home and both the fortifications and State Rooms at Warwick are worth inspection. The formal gardens include Victorian Rose Gardens and a Conservatory. The 60 acres of grounds include nature trails and river walks. Many of the castle's rooms contain exhibitions and displays including medieval armour and reconstructions by Madame

HISTORIC BUILDINGS

Tussaud's. There is a restaurant, catering and picnic areas. Warwick Castle is the most visited stately home in Britain.

Open every day except Christmas Day.

☎ 0926 495421

SEE ALSO *PARKS AND GARDENS* AND *THE REGION AT PLAY*

Weston Park
Near Shifnal, Shropshire

The house was built in early Restoration style by Lady Wilbraham in 1671. It contains impressive collections of furniture and tapestries and is particularly famous for its collection of fine art. The parklands were designed by Capability Brown and include a deer park and woodlands with walks. Attractions in the grounds include a miniature railway, tropical house and an adventure playground. There is a bar, a tea room and picnic areas.

Open daily in August, every day except Mondays and Fridays in June and July and all weekends and Bank Holidays between Easter and the end of September.

☎ 095 276 207

SEE ALSO *PARKS AND GARDENS* AND *THE REGION AT PLAY*

HISTORIC BUILDINGS

Wightwick Manor
Wightwick, near Wolverhampton, West Midlands

The Manor is only just over 100 years old, having been constructed in 1887 but is a major example of the work and influence of William Morris. It contains many original Morris wallpapers and fabrics as well as other Pre-Raphaelite work such as Kempe glass and de Morgan ware. The terraced gardens make much use of Yew and are fine examples of a Victorian/Edwardian garden.

Open on Thursdays, Saturdays and Bank Holiday Sundays and Mondays between March and the end of December.

☎ 0902 761108

Wilderhope Manor
Near Much Wenlock, Shropshire

The National Trust maintains this 16th century manor. Built of local limestone, it was constructed in 1586 and has remained unaltered since. It is set in remote wooded country on the slopes of Wenlock Edge.

Open on Saturdays all year and Wednesdays between April and September.

☎ 06943 363

A rare aerial view of the stronghold and stately home of Warwick Castle

RELIGIOUS BUILDINGS

Birmingham Cathedral
Central Birmingham, West Midlands

A classic example of a Palladian style building, a style rarely featured in religious buildings. The cathedral contains four windows illustrating the keys stages of the life of Christ [Nativity, Crucifixion, Ascension and Judgement], they were designed by Sir Edward Burne-Jones and executed by William Morris.

Open every day

☎ 021 236 4333

Coventry Cathedral
Coventry, West Midlands

The present cathedral was built in 1962 alongside the ruins of 14th century St. Michael's. It contains some of the most outstanding religious art of the second half of the 20th century including Jacob Epstein's sculpture of St. Michael and the Devil, John Piper's Baptistry Window and Graham Sutherland's masterpiece tapestry of Christ in his Majesty.

Open every day

☎ 0203 227597

RELIGIOUS BUILDINGS

Gloucester Cathedral
Gloucester, Gloucestershire

The present cathedral buildings date from 1089 onwards. The Great East Window was built in 1350 to commemorate the Battle of Crecy, measuring 72 feet by 38 feet it is the largest single stained glass window in Britain. The building's finest architecture includes the Perpendicular choir and the fan vaulting in the Cloister. The cathedral also contains Edward II's tomb and it was in the Chapter House that William the Conqueror ordered the creation of the Domesday Book.

Open all year.

☎ 0452 528095

Hailes Abbey
Stanway, near Winchcombe, Gloucestershire

The extensive ruins of a Cistercian abbey founded in 1246 by Richard Earl of Cornwall, King John's son. Jointly managed by English Heritage and the National Trust it also houses a museum of the Abbey's excavations and a shop.

Open Tuesday to Sunday in Winter and every day during the Summer.

☎ No telephone.

New and old side by side at Coventry Cathedral

RELIGIOUS BUILDINGS

Hereford Cathedral
Hereford, Herefordshire

The Cathedral's architecture represents a mixture of styles from Norman onwards. The cathedral contains two world-famous treasures. The Mappa Mundi is a rare early map of the known world, centred on Jerusalem it was drawn on vellum by Richard di Bello in 1289. The Hereford Chained Library is the largest in the world, containing 1,440 books including 8th century illuminated Gospels.

The cathedral is open all year, the Chained Library is closed on Sundays.

☎ 0432 59880

Hereford Cathedral

Holy Trinity Church
Stratford-upon-Avon, Warwickshire

Stratford's parish church on the banks of the River Avon. Regarded by many as one of the most beautiful parish churches in England. Most famous as the burial place of William Shakespeare, Anne Hathaway and other members of the Shakespeare family.

RELIGIOUS BUILDINGS

Open all year except on Christmas Day, Boxing Day and New Years Day.

☎ 0789 266316

Lichfield Cathedral
Lichfield, Staffordshire

One of the most beautiful medieval cathedral's in Britain, it is unique in having three spires. The Flemish glasswork in the Lady Chapel is particularly fine. Amongst its treasures is an 8th century manuscript of the Gospels.

Open every day

☎ 0543 250300

St. Chad's Cathedral
St. Chad's Circus, Birmingham, West Midlands

A Neo-Gothic building showing strong teutonic influences, the cathedral was created by the great Victorian Gothic designer Pugin. It has twin spires. The interior contains Flemish carvings and stained glass executed by John Hardman.

Open every day.

☎ 021 236 2251

Shrewsbury Abbey
Shrewsbury, Shropshire

A Benedictine Abbey founded in 1083 by Roger de Montgomery. It was dissolved by Henry VIII and destroyed apart from the Abbey Church which, although damaged, was saved by the townspeople. The Victorians enlarged the church and built in a style which reflected and enhanced the simple Norman style of the Nave.

Open every day.

☎ No telephone number.

RELIGIOUS BUILDINGS

Tewkesbury Abbey
Tewkesbury, Gloucestershire

The present Abbey was consecrated in 1121 although there has been a church on the site for over 1,200 years. The Abbey is a fine example of the Romanesque and Decorated style of Gothic architecture. It was the last abbey to be dissolved by Henry VIII and the abbey church was saved when the townspeople of Tewkesbury paid £453 to buy it from the king.

Open all year.

☎ 0684 850959

Tintern Abbey
Tintern, Gloucestershire

The abbey was built in 1311 by Cistercian monks on a site at a bend in the River Wye. The ruins are totally roofless but the architectural quality of the stonework and the beautiful position in the Wye Valley make them one of the most romantic and photogenic in Britain.

Open all year.

☎ No telephone.

Worcester Cathedral
Worcester, Worcestershire

The cathedral is beautifully positioned alongside the River Severn and reflects a variety of architectural styles as it was constructed, enlarged and altered for over 500 years following its foundation in the 11th century. It contains the tomb of King John. He died in 1216 and his tomb was erected in 1232, it is made of Purbeck Marble and is surmounted by an effigy of the King. The effigy was made in 1218 and is the oldest surviving royal effigy in the country.

Open every day.

☎ 0905 28854

MUSEUMS & ART GALLERIES

Aerospace Museum

Cosford, Shropshire

A large and varied collection of aircraft, rockets and missiles. There are also displays of different types of aero engines. The military aircraft include examples of British, American, German and Japanese war planes and there is also a detailed history of civil aviation in Britain. There is a cafeteria and shop and the museum's grounds include picnic areas.

Open every day except for over Christmas.

☎ 0902 374872

Avoncroft Museum of Buildings

Stoke Heath, near Bromsgrove, Worcestershire

A large collection of historic buildings that have been saved from destruction, moved to Avoncroft and re-built. The buildings include a 15th century timber-framed house, a Georgian ice house, a 19th century toll house, a chain-making workshop, a barn, a windmill and a dovecote.

Open between March and November except for Mondays and Fridays, open every day in June, July and August.

☎ 0527 31886

Bass Museum

Burton-upon-Trent, Staffordshire

The history of the brewing town of Burton-upon-Trent and the world-famous Bass Brewery. Exhibits include a model of Burton-upon-Trent as it appeared in the early 1920s, an Edwardian bar, a Brewhouse, steam engines and Bass' historic fleet of both horse drawn and powered lorries and drays. The museum is also the home of the famous Bass Shire Horses. Facilities include a bar, a restaurant and a shop.

MUSEUMS & ART GALLERIES

Open every day except Christmas Day, Boxing Day and New Years Day.

☎ 0283 511000

Black Country Museum

Dudley, West Midlands

An open area museum depicting the story of the country's industrial heartland in its heyday. A wide range of buildings have been moved and re-built on the 26 acre site including workshops, a chemists, general shops, a chapel and houses. There is also a canal and a working electric tramway. The complex includes a working period public house and a restaurant.

Open daily between March and October, open Wednesday to Sunday in Winter.

☎ 021 557 9643

The Bass Museum is the home of the famous Shire Horses

MUSEUMS & ART GALLERIES

Blists Hill Open Air Museum
Ironbridge, Shropshire

Ironbridge is the birthplace of the Industrial Revolution and Blists Hill recreates a Victorian working town at the height of the British Empire. All the locations in the museum are authentically restored, stocked with period goods and staffed by workers in the appropriate dress of the era. The locations include the only working wrought ironworks in the developed world, two blast furnaces, a saw mill, printing shop, toll house, sweet shop, chemist's shop, bakers, pub, bank, church and squatter's cottage.

Open all year except Christmas Eve and Christmas Day.

☎ 0952 433522

Chatterley Whitfield Mining Museum
Near Stoke-on-Trent, Staffordshire

This museum offers visitors the opportunity to travel underground into a coal mine and see for themselves the techniques and

Coalport China Museum

MUSEUMS & ART GALLERIES

equipment used in coal mining, both today and in the past. It also houses the British Coal Collection. There are pit ponies and working steam engines. There is also a working reconstructed 1930s pit canteen.

Open every day.

☎ 0782 813337

Cider Museum
Hereford, Herefordshire

The story of cider making through the centuries. The collection of machinery and artefacts associated with cider production include huge Oak vats from Napoleonic times, a 17th century beam press, original champagne cider cellars and a 1920s bottling line. The museum also features the working King Offa Cider Brandy Distillery and a shop.

Open Mondays to Saturdays in the afternoons between November and March and all day every day for the rest of the year.

☎ 0432 354207

SEE ALSO *FOOD AND DRINK*

MUSEUMS & ART GALLERIES

Coalbrookdale Furnace and Museum of Iron
Ironbridge, Shropshire

In 1709 Abraham Darby discovered a way of smelting iron using coke instead of charcoal and in 1758 his son, Abraham Darby II, founded the world's first blast furnace, the Industrial Revolution had started. The furnace is preserved at Coalbrookdale and the adjoining museum tells the story of iron and steel making.

Open all year except Christmas Eve and Christmas Day.

☎ 0952 433522

Coalport China Museum
Ironbridge, Shropshire

The original Coalport China factory has been converted into a museum offering an insight into the methods of making china and the lives of workers in a china factory. There are also stunning displays of Coalport's finest products.

Open all year except Christmas Eve and Christmas Day.

☎ 0952 433522

Cotswold Motor Museum
Bourton-on-the-Water, Gloucestershire

An 18th century watermill housing a collection of 30 sporting cars and motorbikes from the early years to the 1950s. It also houses a vintage caravan collection and one of the largest collections of advertising signs in Britain, featuring more than 800 signs. The museum also features a village life exhibition with a reconstructed Edwardian village shop and living accommodation.

Closed during December and January

☎ 0451 21255

MUSEUMS & ART GALLERIES

Cotswold Teddy Bear Museum
Broadway, Worcestershire

One of the largest collections of teddy bears in the country. There are also displays of old dolls and toys and there is a shop.

Open every day.

☎ No telephone number.

Elgar's Birthplace
Lower Broadheath, near Worcester, Worcestershire

Edward Elgar was born in this cottage in 1857. The museum houses a great deal of Elgar memorabilia including the manuscript of his Second Symphony.

Closed on Wednesdays and between the middle of January and the middle of February.

☎ 0905 332224

MUSEUMS & ART GALLERIES

Gladstone Pottery Museum
Longton, Stoke on Trent, Staffordshire

This museum has been created in a preserved 19th century pottery. Craftsmen use Victorian equipment to demonstrate the traditional skills of the Staffordshire potters. There are exhibits of tiles, lavatories and baths. Pottery colouring techniques are also explained. There is a gift shop.

Open Mondays to Saturdays from March to October and Tuesdays to Saturdays during the rest of the year.

☎ 0782 319232

Holst's Birthplace Museum
Cheltenham, Gloucestershire

Gustav Holst's life is traced and recreated in the childhood home where he was born in 1874. Individual rooms in the Regency terrace house depict life in Victorian and Edwardian times and the collection includes

MUSEUMS & ART GALLERIES

Holst's piano and original manuscripts of his works.

Closed on Sundays, Mondays and all Bank Holidays.

☎ 0242 524826

Ironbridge Gorge Museum
Ironbridge, Shropshire

The story of the area's most famous family of Ironmasters, the Darbys, culminates with the work of Abraham Darby III. Building on the creative genius of his grandfather and the industrial prowess of his father he used their skills to build the world's first iron bridge. Opened in 1779 it still spans the River Severn at Coalbrookdale and, appropriately enough, is called Ironbridge. The museum tells the story of the Industrial Revolution.

Open all year except Christmas Eve and Christmas Day.

☎ 0952 433522

Ironbridge is the home of the world's first bridge constructed of iron

MUSEUMS & ART GALLERIES

Izaak Walton Cottage Museum
Shallowford, near Stone, Staffordshire

Izaak Walton wrote The Compleat Angler and lived in this black and white Staffordshire cottage. It has been converted into a museum displaying his life, times and work. The grounds include a period herb garden and a picnic orchard.

Open every day except Mondays between April and October and at weekends in March and November.

☎ 0785 760278

Jackfield Tile Museum
Ironbridge, Shropshire

The site of the Craven Dunnill factory, once one of he world's leading tile manufacturing plants, now houses this museum of 19th century ceramic tiles. There is also an opportunity to see how ceramic tiles are manufactured.

Open all year except Christmas Eve and Christmas Day.

☎ 0952 433522

James Gilbert Rugby Football Museum
Rugby, Warwickshire

Gilbert's have been making world-famous rugby balls since 1842. This museum of rugby memorabilia is housed within their premises.

Open Monday to Saturday all year.

☎ 0788 536500

Jenner Museum
Berkeley, Gloucestershire

This museum is dedicated to the

MUSEUMS & ART GALLERIES

work of Dr. Edward Jenner, discoverer of the smallpox vaccine, and occupies the Georgian house where he lived and worked. The gardens include the Temple of Vaccinia where he injected and treated the poor.

Restricted opening hours, please telephone for details.

☎ 0483 810631

Lost Street Museum
Ross-on-Wye, Herefordshire

A reconstructed Edwardian shopping street containing 10 shops. The appearance of the shops and their authentic goods range from the 1890s to the 1930s and include toys, gramophones, motorbikes and radios. The street and the shops are decorated with thousands of old advertising posters and signs.

Open Fridays, Saturdays and

MUSEUMS & ART GALLERIES

Sundays in December and January and every day for the rest of the year.

☎ 0989 62752

Midland Air Museum
Baginton, near Coventry, West Midlands

The site adjoins Coventry Airport and contains more than 20 major military aircraft including examples of the Lightning fighter and Canberra and Vulcan bombers. The museum also houses the Sir Frank Whittle Jet Heritage Centre with displays of a variety of aero engines and examples of important early jet planes such as the Meteor. There is a shop and cafe and picnic sites.

Open at weekends during the Winter and daily from April to October.

☎ 0203 301033

A typical display room at the Jackfield Tile Museum

MUSEUMS & ART GALLERIES **MUSEUMS & ART GALLERIES** **MUSEUMS & ART GALLERIES**

Museum of British Road Transport
Coventry, West Midlands

One of the greatest museum's in the world devoted entirely to road transport. The history of road transport in this country is told through displays featuring 150 cars, 75 motorcycles and 200 bicycles.

Open every day except Christmas and Boxing Days.

☎ 0203 832425

National Motorcycle Museum
Bickenhill, near Birmingham, West Midlands

The definitive story of British motorcycles and the motorcycle industry is told in this purpose built museum. There are more than 600 British made machines on display covering the 100 year history of the motorcycle from the 1890s to the present day. There is a restaurant at the museum.

Open every day except Christmas and Boxing Days.

☎ 06755 3311

National Waterways Museum
Gloucester Docks, Gloucester, Gloucestershire

The collection is displayed in the Llanthony Warehouse and the adjoining dock and displays the 200-year history of canals and waterways in Britain. It was the 1991 Museum of the Year and features displays of historic boats, working machinery and archive film and sound footage. There is a shop and cafe.

Closed on Christmas Day.

☎ 0452 307009

Nature in Art - The International Centre for Wildlife Art
Twigworth, Gloucestershire

A unique collection of wildlife art in

A display of packaging at the Robert Opie Collection

all media housed in a Georgian mansion dating from 1740. The collection contains representative work from across the world ranging from traditional wildlife scenes to modern abstracts. The Centre also has artists in residence, a nature garden to encourage visitors to attempt their own work, a play area for children and a coffee shop.

Closed over Christmas and Mondays except Bank Holidays.

☎ 0452 731422

Robert Opie Collection - The Museum of Advertising and Packaging
Gloucester Docks, Gloucester, Gloucestershire

The collection is the result of a lifetime devoted to collecting classic examples of advertising and packaging over the last 100 years and

includes posters, enamel signs, tins and boxes. The greatest and most loved TV adverts are also screened continuously. There is a shop and a tea room.

Open every day during the Summer and Tuesday to Sunday in the Winter.

☎ 0452 302309

Warwick Doll Museum
Warwick, Warwickshire

Housed in a building constructed around 1550 this is a unique collection of antique dolls and doll's houses. The exhibits also include toys, books, automata and prams.

Open daily between Easter and the end of September and during School Holidays.

☎ 0926 495546

WORKING ATTRACTIONS

Annard Woollen Mill
Church Lench, near Evesham, Worcestershire

A working woollen mill specialising in producing garments made from mohair. Tour the mill and see the machinery at work before visiting the mill shop. There is also a tea room.

Open every day except Christmas and Boxing Days.

☎ 0386 870270

Berkeley Power Station
Berkeley, Gloucestershire

The first nuclear power station in Great Britain to be de-commissioned. There are guided tours of the reactor and the generators and exhibitions about nuclear power generation.

Weekdays only except by appointment; all children must be 8 years or older and accompanied.

☎ 0453 810431

Brindley Mill

WORKING ATTRACTIONS

Brindley Mill
Leek, Staffordshire

This corn mill was designed by the inventor and engineer James Brindley. It was restored in the early 1970s and is now in full working order. The mill also contains a museum of the life of Brindley and a guide to millwrighting.

Open at weekends and Bank Holidays from Easter to October and also Monday, Tuesday and Wednesday in July and August.

☎ 0538 381000

Brooklyn Farm and Craft Workshop
Waterfall, near Stoke on Trent, Staffordshire

The farm is home to a flock of British Friesland Milking Sheep. The craft workshop's looms and other equipment use the ewes' wool and can be examined as can the rugs, wall hangings and knitwear that they are used to produce. The farm sells the ewes' milk and yoghurt and cheese produced from it.

WORKING ATTRACTIONS

Please telephone for opening times.

☎ 0538 308462

SEE ALSO *FOOD AND DRINK*

Coalport Minerva Works

Fenton, Stoke on Trent, Staffordshire

Guided tours of the Coalport factory to see how fine bone china is made, fired and decorated. There is also a craft centre and shop.

Open Monday to Thursday and Friday mornings all year, tours must be booked in advance although the craft centre and shop can be visited without booking.

☎ 0782 45274

Conderton Pottery

Conderton, near Tewksbury, Gloucestershire

Visitors can watch Toff Milway at work in the Old Forge pottery producing a wide range of country-style pots in his distinctive stoneware. The adjoining Gallery sells earlier examples of Toff's work.

Closed on Sundays and over Christmas.

☎ 0386 89387

Cotswold Perfumery

Bourton-on-the-Water, Gloucestershire

An opportunity to watch perfume being manufactured in the Perfume Compounding Room, a Perfume Garden and an Exhibition of Perfumery which features smelly-vision. There is also a shop selling the perfumes produced on the premises.

Open all year

☎ 0451 20698

Cotswold Woollen Weavers

Filkins, near Lechlade, Gloucestershire

The 18th century mill buildings are used to display the history of weaving in the Cotswolds and show early mill machinery at work. The mill shop offers a wide range of woollen goods and there is also a coffee shop and picnic area.

Open all year, Sundays afternoons only.

☎ 0367 860491

Edinburgh Crystal Factory Shop and Museum

Stourbridge, West Midlands

The factory shop and museum has displays of the work of many of the fine glassware artists who have worked with the company. The complete manufacturing process is shown on an audio-visual presentation.

Open all year except over Christmas and New Year.

☎ 0384 392521

Glassbarn

Newent, Gloucestershire

A small glassworks with viewing gallery. Craftsmen blow and fashion glass into items ranging from goblets and tankards to vases and paperweights. All the glassware can be purchased in the adjoining shop.

Closed on Saturday afternoons and all day on Sundays.

☎ 0531 821173

Jinney Ring Craft Centre

Hanbury, near Bromsgrove, Worcestershire

A series of timbered barns have been restored and converted into workshops at the Jinney Ring Centre. Craftsmen in the workshops demonstrate a wide range of rural and artistic skills including pottery, jewellery making, painting, glass cutting and knitting. The Centre has an exhibition gallery and gift shop and a restaurant.

Open all year.

☎ 0527 821653

Prinknash Abbey Pottery

Painswick, Gloucestershire

Viewing gallery and shop of world famous pottery of Benedictine Abbey. Watch local craftsmen at work on pots before buying similar ones from the shop.

Open every day.

☎ 0452 812239

Royal Brierley Crystal

Brierley Hill, Birmingham, West Midlands

Guided tours of the Royal Brierley factory and private museum. There is a factory shop and a restaurant.

Open every day apart from Public Holidays.

☎ 0384 70161

Royal Doulton

Burslem, Stoke on Trent, Staffordshire

Tours of the Royal Doulton factory showing the manufacturing processes for both figures and tableware. Also the Sir Henry Doulton Gallery which contains a Doulton museum, shop and cafe.

Open Monday to Friday all year but it is advisable to book tour places in advance.

☎ 0782 575454

Royal Doulton Crystal

Stourbridge, West Midlands

Royal Doulton's Webb Corbett Glassworks still produces fine English crystal by traditional methods and the guided tour shows these skills through all the stages of manufacture. There is also a shop.

Tours from Monday to Friday, the shop is also open on Saturdays.

☎ 0834 440442

WORKING ATTRACTIONS

Royal Grafton China
Longton, Stoke on Trent, Staffordshire

Guided tour of the Royal Grafton factory showing the manufacturing processes for both tableware and giftware. There is a factory shop.

Open for tours Monday to Friday all year but they must be booked in advance.

☎ 0782 599667

Royal Worcester
Worcester, Worcestershire

The factory tour demonstrates the making of fine porcelain. The museum contains samples of some of Royal Worcester's greatest work. There is also a showroom and shop.

Open Monday to Saturday all year.

☎ 0905 23221

Spode Works
Stoke on Trent, Staffordshire

Tours including a guided visit to the Spode museum and a look at all the processes involved in making bone china. There is a shop and catering facilities.

WORKING ATTRACTIONS

Tours all year Monday to Thursday and Friday mornings, but they must be booked in advance.

☎ 0782 744011

Wedgwood Visitor Centre
Barlaston, near Stoke on Trent, Staffordshire

Wedgwood craftsmen demonstrate the art of making and decorating fine china. There is also a museum, art gallery, shop and catering facilities.

Open Monday to Saturday during November to Easter and every day for the rest of the year.

☎ 0782 204141

Winchcombe Pottery
Near Winchcombe, Gloucestershire

A centre for a variety of crafts and craftsmen. The centrepiece is the pottery with its historic bottle kiln. Handmade pots from the pottery can be purchased at the shop. Other craftsmen working on the site include an upholsterer, jeweller, cabinet maker, sculptor and decorative painter.

Open all year.

☎ 0242 602462

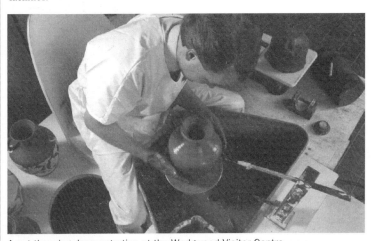

A pot throwing demonstration at the Wedgwood Visitor Centre

STEAM RAILWAYS

Birmingham Railway Museum

Tyseley, Birmingham, West Midlands

A converted GWR engine shed houses the collection of 12 steam locomotives and a variety of coaches and other rolling stock including two Royal Saloons. Restoration work can be inspected in the engineering workshops. The locomotives are often in steam and give visitors demonstration rides. Refreshments are available.

Open every day, steam days are Sundays, normally twice a month please telephone for exact days.

☎ 021 707 4696

Cheddleton Railway Centre

Cheddleton, near Leek, Staffordshire

Based around a Victorian railway station the centre's static display features both steam and diesel engines as well as coaches and other rolling stock. The station also has a small museum, shop and refreshments room. On steam days the locomotives offer short trips. The centre also organises many special events.

The Centre is open on Sundays only between October and March and every day for the rest of the year. Please telephone for details on steam days and special events.

☎ 0538 360522

Dean Forest Railway

Near Lydney, Gloucestershire

Static displays of steam engines, diesel engines, coaches and wagons and a collection of railwayana. During steam days the engines are fired up and take visitors on short rides.

Displays open every day, steam days on Sundays during the Summer, Bank Holidays and Wednesdays between June and August.

☎ 0594 843423

STEAM RAILWAYS

Didcot Railway Centre

Didcot, Oxfordshire

A major collection of steam locomotives, coaches and rolling stock from the old Great Western Railway. There is also a reconstruction of Isambard Kingdom Brunel's original large-gauge tracks and carriages which the GWR tried to use before standardisation of gauges occurred. In addition to the static displays there are regular steam days. Refreshments are available.

Static display open all year, please telephone for information on steam days.

☎ 0235 817200

Foxfield Steam Railway

Stoke on Trent, Staffordshire

Foxfield offers a 5 mile round trip steam ride through the Staffordshire countryside.

Open from Easter to September on Sundays and on Saturday, Sunday and Monday on Bank Holiday weekends during the opening period.

☎ 0782 396210

Gloucester and Warwickshire Steam Railway

Toddington Station, near Cheltenham, Gloucestershire

Restored GWR station with signal box, goods yard, locomotive sheds and displays of engines and rolling stock. The working line runs for about 4 miles to Gretton with a stop at the newly restored Winchcombe station. Toddington Station is also home to a steam-hauled narrow-gauge railway, the North Gloucestershire Railway, and has a restaurant.

STEAM RAILWAYS

Station and displays open all year, steam days at weekends and Bank Holidays during the Summer.

☎ 0242 621405

Severn Valley Railway

Bridgnorth, Shropshire

The Severn Valley Railway runs for 16 miles from Bridgnorth to Kidderminster, there are 6 stations along the line. Bridgnorth Station houses the UK's largest collection of standard gauge steam and diesel engines. The railway is in steam every weekend during the Summer and other facilities at Bridgnorth include a railway gift shop and a range of refreshments including a real ale pub, appropriately named The Railwaymen's Arms.

Station open all year, steam days every Saturday and Sunday from mid-May to early October and every Bank Holiday during the Summer.

☎ 0299 403816

The branch line in steam at the Didcot Railway Centre

Acton Scott Historic Working Farm

Acton Scott, near Church Stretton, Shropshire

A very unusual working farm dedicated to preserving and using 19th century farming methods. Heavy horses are used rather than tractors and all the work on the farm is undertaken without using the help of electricity or the petrol engine. Traditional country crafts are demonstrated on the farm and its produce is for sale.

Open April to the end of October except for Mondays.

☎ 06946 306

Amerton Working Farm

Stowe-by-Chartley, near Stafford, Staffordshire

A dairy farm with a herd of pedigree Jersey cows. Visitors can see day-to-day farm work, feeding the animals and milking as well as cheese and ice cream making. The farm also has a craft shop, bakery, garden centre and farm shop. There is a tea room and a picnic area.

Open every day

☎ 0889 270294

Brooklyn Farm and Craft Workshop

Waterfall, near Stoke on Trent, Staffordshire

A 10 acre farm working a flock of British Friesland Milking Sheep. The day-to-day workings of the farm including the milking can be watched as can the manufacture of yoghurt and cheese from the ewes' milk. The craft workshop's looms and other equipment use the ewes' wool and can be examined as can the rugs, wall hangings and knitwear that they are used to produce.

Please telephone for opening times.

☎ 0538 308462

SEE ALSO *WORKING ATTRACTIONS*

Cadbury World

Bournville, Birmingham, West Midlands

Constructed on part of the Cadbury factory in Bournville Cadbury World tells the history of chocolate and the story of the Cadbury company. It also tells why George and Richard Cadbury decided to leave the city and build their new factory in Bournville and presents a picture of life in Bournville in the 1920s. Many of Cadbury's TV advertisements are famous and you can also relive some of the reasons why ..the lady loves Milk Tray. There is also a demonstration area where visitors can see sample chocolates being made and a tour of the modern packaging plant. There is also a shop and restaurant.

Open every day except Christmas Day.

☎ 021 433 4334

Children's Farm

Middleton, near Tamworth, Staffordshire

Devoted to introducing children to the joys of farming and animal husbandry. There are friendly farm animals, rare breeds and shire horses. The farm has play areas and picnic barns and can organise special events for birthdays.

Open all year.

☎ No telephone number.

Cider Museum and King Offa Distillery

Hereford, Herefordshire

The King Offa Distillery is a working distillery producing cider brandy. There is an off-licence and gift shop

FOOD & DRINK

attached to it. The museum tells the story of cider making through the centuries and contains a large collection of machinery and artefacts associated with cider production.

Open Mondays to Saturdays in the afternoons between November and March and all day every day for the rest of the year.

☎ 0432 354207

SEE ALSO *MUSEUMS AND ART GALLERIES.*

HP Bulmer Drinks
Hereford, Herefordshire

Tours of the Bulmer cider factory including the bottling plant, vat house and sample room. The Strongbow Vat is almost 65 feet tall and 76 feet in diameter, it holds 1,630,000 gallons of cider and is reputedly the largest vat in the world.

Open weekdays all year with three tours per day, you must book places on a tour in advance.

☎ 0432 352000

Hop Pocket Hop Farm
Near Bishops Frome, Herefordshire

One of few remaining working hop farms in the Heart of England. Depending on the time of year visitors can see the entire process of growing and picking hops. At harvest time the farm uses one of the largest sets of hop picking machines in the country and also has amongst the largest drying kilns. The farm also cultivates other crops and keeps sheep. There is a craft shop offering work from an extensive range of local craftsmen.

Open weekends only between January and March and Tuesdays to Sundays during the rest of the year.

☎ 053186 323

FOOD & DRINK

Hoo Farm Country Park
Hoo, Preston-on-the-Weald Moors, near Telford, Shropshire

A traditional Shropshire working farm which specialises in preserving old country skills such as bee keeping, pheasant rearing and trout rearing. You can also see the farm's sheep being sheared and the wool being spun and weaved. There is a farm trail, tea room and shop.

Open Tuesdays to Sundays between early May and early September.

☎ 0952 677917

St. Augustine's Farm
Arlingham, Gloucestershire

124 acres farm around a bend in the River Severn. A wide range of farm animals including cows, goats, sheep, pigs and chicken. Watch the farm at work or walk the farm trail. There is

FOOD & DRINK

also a display of early agricultural equipment, a children's play area and a tea and gift shop.

Only open during the summer unless by prior appointment

☎ 0452 740277

Sandwell Park Farm
Sandwell, near West Bromwich, West Midlands

Part of the Earl of Dartmouth's estate has been converted into a working farm practising 19th century farming methods. There are displays of rare breeds and demonstrations of farming techniques. There is also a farm trail. The farm has a country crafts centre and a shop. There are tea rooms and picnic sites.

Open every day.

☎ 021 553 0220

An unusual shot of the cider vats at HP Bulmer Drinks

FOOD & DRINK

Shugborough Estate

Home Farm Milford, near Stafford, Staffordshire

The ancestral home of the Earls of Lichfield Shugborough Hall is an 18th century mansion set in a 900 acre estate. The estate's Home Farm is being used as a working 19th century farm with rare breeds and a restored corn mill. There are regular demonstrations of traditional farming methods. There is also a special area of the farm, Noah's Park, devoted to introducing children to farm animals. The estate also includes the Staffordshire County Museum. There are tea rooms, a shop and picnic areas.

Open every day between the end of March and the End of October.

☎ 0889 881388

SEE ALSO *PARKS AND GARDENS* AND *HISTORIC BUILDINGS*

FOOD & DRINK

Three Choirs Vineyard

Near Newent, Gloucestershire

The home of Three Choirs English Wine, casual visitors are welcome to look around the vineyard and winery and sample the wines. Conducted tours including a wine-tasting and lunch or supper are also organised but must be booked in advance.

Open weekdays only between Christmas and Easter, every day for the rest of the year.

☎ 053185 223

Umberslade Children's Farm

Tanworth-in-Arden, near Solihull, Warwickshire

Part of a large commercial Warwickshire farm has been developed to show children what life is like on a real farm. Visitors can see the daily work of the farm and observe all of the wide variety of

WILDLIFE

animals on the farm. The farm shop sells a wide range of the farm's products including goat's milk and cheese. There is also a play area and a picnic area.

Open daily from the end of March to the end of October.

☎ 05644 2251

Three Choirs Vineyard

WILDLIFE

Batsford Park Falconry Centre

Batsford, near Moreton-in-the-Marsh, Gloucestershire

The Centre houses more than 70 birds of prey. As well as falcons there are also eagles, hawks and owls. Regular flying demonstrations are organised and there are breeding aviaries and woodland walks. Batsford Park also contains the Batsford Park Arboretum.

Open mid-March to November.

☎ 0386 701043

SEE ALSO *PARKS AND GARDENS*

Birdland

Bourton-on-the-Water, Gloucestershire

World-famous bird gardens along the banks of the River Windrush. It includes a centre for protecting endangered species of birds from around the world and has an active and successful breeding programme for these rare breeds. The gardens also contain many species of wildfowl and a Penguin Rookery which is unique in Britain.

Open all year.

☎ 0451 20480

Birtsmorton Waterfowl Sanctuary

Birtsmorton, near Malvern, Worcestershire

The sanctuary covers 7 acres and is home to around 80 species of waterfowl including swans, geese and ducks. Visitors can enjoy walking amongst the birds in their natural habitat and can feed them.

Open every day except Christmas Day.

☎ 068 481 376

WILDLIFE

Blackbrook Animal and Bird World

Winkhill, near Leek, Staffordshire

A collection of rare breeds of farm animals. The are also various exotic bird species as well as pheasants and waterfowl. The breeding programme means that at the right times of the year there are baby animals on view and there is also a pets corner. There is a shop and a picnic area.

Open every day except Wednesdays from Easter to the end of September.

☎ 0538 308293

Coombe Abbey Country Park

Near Coventry, West Midlands

The 372 acre site includes a major, nationally recognised nature reserve and an important birdwatching site with hides. There are also formal gardens and fishing in the lake.

Open all year.

☎ 0203 453720

Cotswold Farm Park Rare Breeds Centre

Guiting Power, near Bourton-on-the-Water, Gloucestershire

The Centre houses the largest collection of rare farm breeds in Britain and offers seasonal exhibits of farming life. It also features a farm trail, adventure playground, pets corner, shop and cafe.

Open April to September.

☎ 0451 850307

SEE ALSO *THE REGION AT PLAY*

WILDLIFE

Addersbury Lakes

Addersbury, near Bloxham, Oxfordshire

The Addersbury Lakes site used to be part of the Duke of Argyll's estate and was landscaped by Capability Brown. It has now been converted into a nature reserve. The two lakes have islands in them and the reserve is home to a wide range of wildlife including Muntjac deer and Kingfishers.

Open all year.

☎ 0295 870312

WILDLIFE

Cotswold Wildlife Park
Near Burford, Oxfordshire

The park spreads over 120 acres and includes wildlife from across the world including white rhinos, tigers and leopards. There is also a butterfly house, a reptile house and an aquarium and the grounds also include picnic areas, a narrow-gauge railway, a brass-rubbing centre and an adventure playground.

Closed on Christmas Day

☎ 0993 823006

SEE ALSO *THE REGION AT PLAY*

Domestic Fowl Trust
Honeybourne, near Evesham, Worcestershire

A unique collection of 150 different breeds of turkey, geese, ducks and chickens. The Trust also runs a children's farm and has an adventure playground. There is a tea room and a gift shop.

Open all year round except Fridays.

☎ 0386 833083

WILDLIFE

Drayton Manor Park and Zoo
Near Tamworth, Staffordshire

A leisure complex spread over 160 acres including a zoo and zoo farm. There are also more than 50 rides and attractions, a garden centre, shops and restaurants.

Open every day from Easter to October.

☎ 0827 287979

SEE ALSO *THE REGION AT PLAY*

Dudley Zoo and Castle
Dudley, West Midlands

The Zoo spreads over 40 acres of gardens and woodlands and holds approximately 1,000 animals in well-planned environments. The site also includes the ruins of Dudley Castle, an amusement park and children's adventure playground. There is a cafeteria.

Open except for Christmas Day.

☎ 0384 252401

SEE ALSO *THE REGION AT PLAY*

Dudley Zoo and Castle offers family enjoyment in a superb setting

WILDLIFE

Falconry Centre
Hagley, near Kidderminster, Worcestershire

The Centre is the home to many birds of prey. In addition to falcons there are eagles, hawks and owls. There are regular falconry displays and the Centre runs courses. There is a gift shop.

Open every day except Christmas and Boxing Days.

☎ 0562 700014

Folly Farm Waterfowl
Bourton-on-the-Water, Gloucestershire

A conservation centre for more than 160 species of wildfowl and waterfowl created on a 50 acre Cotswold farm with lakes and other natural environments. There are also farm animals and an undercover pets area.

Open all year.

☎ 0451 20285

The Mere
Ellesmere, Shropshire

The area is famous for its wildfowl and the Mere offers a large space for them to gather. There are hides and a visitor centre providing information on the birds and also on the area's geology, fauna and flora. The centre also has a bird observatory and sales area. Parts of the Mere are also used for fishing and boating and the surrounding area has sporting facilities.

Open all year, the visitor centre is open in the afternoons from Easter to the end of October.

☎ 0743 252362

SEE ALSO *THE REGION AT PLAY*

WILDLIFE

Moorlands Farm Park of British Rare Breeds
Near Stoke on Trent, Staffordshire

More than 70 rare breeds of cattle, sheep and pigs are cared for a Moorlands. There is also a pets corner and a children's play area. There is a shop where light refreshments are available in addition to a picnic area.

Open every day between April and November.

☎ 0538 266479

National Birds of Prey Centre
Newent, Gloucestershire

The largest collection of birds of prey in western Europe featuring eagles, falcons, hawks, owls and vultures. Daily flying exhibitions. The Centre also includes breeding aviaries and a coffee shop.

Open February to November.

☎ 0531 820286

Prinknash Bird Park
Near Painswick, Gloucestershire

The park is the home of a wide variety of bird life including peacocks, cranes, swans and pheasants as well as flocks of Fallow Deer and goats. A walk through the woods leads to the Haunted Monks Fish Pond which is full of trout.

Open every day.

☎ 0452 812727

Stratford-upon-Avon Butterfly Farm
Stratford-upon-Avon, Warwickshire

Europe's largest live butterfly collection. There are hundreds of butterflies from all around the world

WILDLIFE

and they fly around in a specially constructed tropical environment planted with exotic trees and plants. The farm also has a collection of spiders and scorpions including what is reputedly the largest spider in the world.

Open every day.

☎ 0789 299288

Stratford-upon-Avon Shire Horse Centre
Near Stratford-upon-Avon, Warwickshire

The shire horses at the Centre perform day-to-day work on the farm. It also has many rare breeds of farm animals as well as riverside walks, a pets corner, an adventure playground, tea gardens and a shop.

Open all year.

☎ 0789 266276

Twycross Zoo
Near Twycross, Warwickshire

Twycross houses the finest collection of monkeys and other primates in the country. It is also the home of examples of many of the world's endangered species and has an impressive reptile house. There is a children's adventure playground.

Open all year except Christmas Day.

☎ 0827 880250

Umberslade Children's Farm
Tanworth-in-Arden, near Solihull, Warwickshire

Part of a large commercial Warwickshire farm has been developed to show children what life is like on a real farm. Visitors can see the daily work of the farm and observe all of the wide variety of

WILDLIFE

animals on the farm. There is also a farm shop, play area and picnic area.

Open daily from the end of March to the end of October.

☎ 05644 2251

SEE ALSO *FOOD AND DRINK*

West Midlands Safari and Leisure Park
Near Bewdley, Worcestershire

The Safari Park area consists of a series of animal reserves. The reserves allow visitors to see the animals in their natural environments. The site also contains a reptile house, a sealion reserve with regular shows and a pets corner. A train takes visitors from the animals to an amusement area with many rides and attractions.

Open daily between April and October.

☎ 0299 402114

SEE ALSO *THE REGION AT PLAY*

A young Pygmy chimp at Twycross Zoo

WILDLIFE

Wildfowl and Wetlands Trust

Slimbridge, Gloucestershire

Slimbridge was founded in 1946 as the first of Sir Peter Scott's trusts and is the largest wildfowl collection in the world. The resident collection is around 3,300 birds from 164 species including around 400 flamingos. This collection is housed in 94 acres of ground and there are a further 800 acres as a temporary refuge for flocks of migrating wildfowl. There are many paths with hides, a gift shop and cafe.

Closed Christmas Eve and Christmas Day.

☎ 0453 890065

Slimbridge

World of Butterflies

Jubilee Park, Symonds Yat West, Herefordshire

A splendid collection of butterflies living and flying freely inside a large tropical-environment glass house. Jubilee park also contains a hedge maze, museum of mazes, craft shops, a garden centre, riverside walks and a variety of refreshments.

Closed in January

☎ 0600 890360

THE REGION AT PLAY

Alton Towers

Alton, near Stoke on Trent, Staffordshire

Britain's largest and most popular theme park. The 200 acres of grounds contain 125 different rides and attractions. Its famous white-knuckle rides include the Corkscrew, the Black Hole, the Grand Canyon Rapids Ride and Thunderlooper, Britain's largest single loop rollercoaster. All types of catering are also available on site.

Open daily from the end of March to early November.

☎ 0538 702200

The Haunted House at Alton Towers

THE REGION AT PLAY

Blenheim Palace

Woodstock, Oxfordshire

The stately home of the Duke of Marlborough. The Palace was designed by Vanbrugh and is one of the finest examples of English Baroque architecture. The State Rooms contain displays of fine furniture, paintings, tapestries and sculpture. The 2,000 acres of surrounding parkland were landscaped by Capability Brown and make magnificent use of water features. There is a garden centre within the park. Attractions at Blenheim include the Winston Churchill exhibition, a narrow-gauge railway, a maze, a butterfly house, a nature trail, boating on the lake and an adventure playground. There are restaurants, cafeterias, picnic spots and a gift shop.

Open daily from mid March until the end of October.

☎ 0993 811325

SEE ALSO *PARKS AND GARDENS* **AND** *HISTORIC BUILDINGS*

Bourton Model Village

Bourton-on-the-Water, Gloucestershire

Created in 1937 from Cotswold stone in the gardens of The Old New Inn, a village public house and hotel, this is a 1/9th scale model of the entire village of Bourton-on-the-Water as it appeared in the 1930s.

Closed on Christmas Day.

☎ 0451 20467

Broadway Tower Country Park

Broadway, Worcestershire

Centred on Broadway's famous folly, a tower erected by the 6th Earl of Coventry in 1793, the Park includes nature walks through countryside full of wildlife, displays of rare breeds of

THE REGION AT PLAY

animals and birds and an adventure playground. Refreshments are available and there are picnic areas in the Park.

Open daily from April to the end of October.

☎ 0386 852390

Cotswold Farm Park Rare Breeds Centre

Guiting Power, near Bourton-on-the-Water, Gloucestershire

The Centre includes a farm trail, adventure playground and pets corner. It houses the largest collection of rare farm breeds in Britain and offers seasonal exhibits of farming life. There is a cafe and a shop.

Open April to September.

☎ 0451 850307

SEE ALSO *WILDLIFE*

Cotswold Water Park

Near Cirencester, Gloucestershire

1,500 acres of grounds containing around 100 lakes provide the

THE REGION AT PLAY

backdrop for a wide range of watersports, fishing and birdwatching. The park also offers nature reserves, walks, horse riding and cycleways.

Open all year.

☎ 0285 861459

Cotswold Wildlife Park

Near Burford, Oxfordshire

A narrow-gauge railway and adventure playground are included in the 200 acres of grounds and the house at the centre of the park houses a brass-rubbing centre, cafeteria and bar. The wildlife comes from across the world and includes white rhinos, leopards, zebras and tigers. There is also a butterfly house, a reptile house, an aquarium and picnic areas.

Closed on Christmas Day

☎ 0993 823006

SEE ALSO *WILDLIFE*

The exciting mine train at Alton Towers

THE REGION AT PLAY

Drayton Manor Park and Zoo

Near Tamworth, Staffordshire

A leisure complex spread over 160 acres of parkland and lakes. There are more than 50 rides and attractions including the famous Pirate Adventure. The complex also includes a zoo, zoo farm, boating lake, garden centre, shops and restaurants.

Open every day from Easter to October.

☎ 0827 287979

SEE ALSO WILDLIFE

Dudley Zoo and Castle

Dudley, West Midlands

The Zoo spreads over 40 acres of gardens and woodlands and holds approximately 1,000 animals in well-planned environments. The site also includes the ruins of Dudley Castle with an audio-visual presentation of the castle's history. There is an amusement park and a children's adventure playground as well as a chairlift. There is a bar and cafeteria.

THE REGION AT PLAY

Open except for Christmas Day.

☎ 0384 252401

SEE ALSO WILDLIFE

Fletchers Country Garden Centre

Eccleshall, Staffordshire

An extensive garden centre with show gardens. There is a craft centre where goods are made and sold, a pets corner and a children's play area. The complex includes an 18-hole continental crazy golf course and licensed tea rooms.

Open every day except Christmas and Boxing Day.

☎ 0785 851067

Gloucester Docks

Gloucester, Gloucestershire

The Victorian docks and warehouses in the centre of Gloucester made the city a major inland port. They have been restored to their full splendour and contain museums, shops and

THE REGION AT PLAY

cafes. There are narrow boat trips around the docks and basins and guided walks around the complex of buildings.

Docks open all year, attractions vary.

☎ 0452 311190

SEE ALSO MUSEUMS AND ART GALLERIES FOR THE MOST IMPORTANT OF THE DOCKS' MUSEUMS.

Hatton Country World

Hatton, near Warwick, Warwickshire

Hatton Country World has the largest craft centre in the country. It also houses a 100 acre farm with more than 40 rare breeds, a children's farm, an adventure playground and a pets corner.

Open all year except for the farm which is open daily between Easter and Christmas.

☎ 0926 843411

Gloucester Docks

THE REGION AT PLAY

House of Tailor of Gloucester
Gloucester, Gloucestershire

The world of Beatrix Potter is brought to life in the building by the cathedral she chose to use to illustrate her Tailor of Gloucester story. The displays include working models bringing the stories to life and a wide range of Potter memorabilia.

Closed on Sundays.

☎ 0452 422856

Himley Model Village
Himley Park, near Dudley, West Midlands

The local world through the centuries is recreated in miniature within a walled garden. Models include Dudley Market Place as it looked in the mid 1800s, Himley Hall, Himley Parish Church and the fictitious village of the Archers, Ambridge. There is also a model yacht marina and a working narrow-gauge railway which visitors can ride on.

Open daily between Easter and the end of October.

☎ 0902 895446

Keith Harding's World of Mechanical Music
Northleach, Gloucestershire

An unusual collection of musical boxes, automata and mechanical musical instruments. There is also a Magical Musical Shop.

Open every day.

☎ 0451 60181

Jubilee Park
Symonds Yat West, Herefordshire

The Jubilee Park complex overlooks a beautiful stretch of the River Wye. Its

THE REGION AT PLAY

many attractions include a famous hedge maze and the world's only museum of mazes, an interactive fun museum especially designed for the young and young at heart. There is also a free-flying butterfly house as well as craft shops, a garden centre, riverside walks and a range of refreshments.

Open all year except for January when only the craft shops and garden centre open.

☎ 0600 890360

SEE ALSO *WILDLIFE*

Kingsbury Water Park
Near Tamworth, Warwickshire

The Water Park covers 600 acres and the lakes offer sailing, windsurfing, hydroplaning, model boating and fishing. There is a nature reserve with

THE REGION AT PLAY

walks. There are also picnic sites, a countryside shop and a cafe.

Closed on Christmas Day.

☎ 0827 872660

The Mere
Ellesmere, Shropshire

The Mere is a large area famous for its wildfowl and there are hides and a visitor centre. It is also used for fishing and boating, both in rowing boats and a power launch. There are also tennis courts, a putting green and a children's playground.

Open all year, the visitor centre is open in the afternoons from Easter to the end of October.

☎ 0743 252362

SEE ALSO *WILDLIFE*

The Jubilee Maze at Jubilee Park

What to see in The Heart of England ....

Ragley Hall
Near Alcester, Warwickshire

The stately home of the Earl of Yarmouth is a Palladian mansion designed by Robert Hooke in 1680. James Gibbs' Great Hall, dating from 1750, is regarded as having the finest Baroque plasterwork in England. The landscaped gardens and park were designed by Capability Brown. There are woodland walks and, for children, an exciting adventure wood and 3-d maze. The lake is equipped with sailing boats. There are picnic places around the lakeshore and a tea room overlooking the Rose Garden.

Open from Easter to the end of September apart from on Mondays [other than Bank Holidays] and Fridays.

☎ 0789 762090

SEE ALSO *PARKS AND GARDENS AND HISTORIC BUILDINGS*

Stratford Brass Rubbing Centre
Stratford-upon-Avon, Warwickshire

Housed in the Summerhouse of the Royal Shakespeare Theatre. The rubbings on display range from characters from Shakespeare's time including Kings, knights, courtiers and merchants to striking Celtic designs. Visitors can make their own brass rubbings, purchase all the equipment they will need and be offered expert guidance.

Open every day from April to October.

☎ 0789 297671

Studley Castle Gardens
Winchcombe, Gloucestershire

Studley Castle is a magnificent Tudor castle surrounded by splendid formal Elizabethan gardens. The castle hosts many craft events where local craftsmen demonstrate their skills. It also hosts a series of special events each year and has a plant centre

selling examples of some of the castle's award winning roses. There is an adventure playground and a restaurant as well as a gift shop.

Open from April to October.

☎ 0242 602308

SEE ALSO *PARKS AND GARDENS AND HISTORIC BUILDINGS*

Trentham Gardens
Trentham, Stoke on Trent, Staffordshire

800 acres of landscaped gardens, parkland and a lake. Watersports are available on the lake as is fly fishing. There is also a clay pigeon shooting facility and a children's adventure playground. The gardens also have a nature reserve and crafts centre. There is a restaurant and a cafe.

Open every day between Easter and October.

☎ 0782 657341

SEE ALSO *PARKS AND GARDENS*

Adventurous watersports on the lake at Trentham Gardens . . .

Twyford Country Centre

Twyford Farm, near Evesham,
Worcestershire

Twyford offers a complete
introduction to the pleasures and
crafts of the countryside. There are
farm trails and riverside walks, a
falconry and wildlife centre, a craft
centre and garden centre and a
miniature railway. There is fishing
both on the River Avon and in the
Centre's Carp Pool. The Centre has a
farm shop and a health food shop and
has a cafe and picnic areas.

Open all year.

☎ 0386 446108

Warwick Castle

Warwick, Warwickshire

Warwick Castle is surrounded by 60
acres of grounds. The gardens
around the castle include a Peacock
Garden, Rose Gardens and a
Conservatory. The rest of the
grounds include woodlands and

feature nature trails, riverside walks
and woodland walks. The present
medieval fortress was created by the
Beauchamp family in the 14th
century. Over the centuries the castle
has served as both a military
stronghold and great baronial stately
home and both the fortifications and
State Rooms at Warwick are worth
inspection. This particularly applies to
the Great Hall, State Rooms,
Armoury, Dungeons, Torture
Chamber and Guy's Tower [named
after Guy Beauchamp who was also
called The Black Dog of Arden].
There are reconstructions using
Madame Tussaud's waxworks,
particularly the tableaux: A Royal
Weekend Party 1898. There is a
restaurant, catering and picnic areas.
Warwick Castle is the most visited
stately home in Britain.

**Open every day except Christmas
Day.**

☎ 0926 495421

**SEE ALSO *HISTORIC BUILDINGS,
AND THE REGION AT PLAY***

West Midlands Safari and Leisure Park

Near Bewdley, Worcestershire

Attractions at the Park include rides
such as the Apple Rollercoaster and
the Pirate Ship. A train takes visitors
from the amusement area to the
animal reserves. The reserves allow
visitors to see the animals in their
natural environments. There is also a
reptile house and a pets corner.

**Open daily between April and
October.**

☎ 0299 402114

SEE ALSO *WILDLIFE*

Weston Park

Near Shifnal, Shropshire

The parklands were designed by
Capability Brown and include a deer
park containing a herd of fallow deer
and flocks of rare breeds of sheep.
Attractions in the grounds include a
miniature railway, a tropical house, a
museum, woodland walks and an
adventure playground. Special events
are held in the grounds throughout
the Summer. The house was built in
early Restoration style in 1671. It
contains impressive collections of
furniture and tapestries and is
particularly famous for its collection
of fine art. There is a bar, a tea room
and picnic areas.

**Open daily in August, every day
except Mondays and Fridays in
June and July and all weekends
and Bank Holidays between
Easter and the end of September.**

☎ 095 276 207

**SEE ALSO *PARKS AND GARDENS
AND HISTORIC BUILDINGS***

. . . or slightly more relaxing fun !

Trentham Gardens
Family days out
page 80

Dudley Zoo
Family days out
page 77

Family days out in

The Heart of England

Nowadays almost all reasonably sized leisure attractions offer facilities and special activities for children and family groups. These can range from an activity or adventure playground in a park or garden to reduced price family tickets and special children's sections in large theme parks.

Some attractions are specifically intended for children and families or offer additional activities during school holidays. Amongst the attractions listed in the main Heart of England listing the following are particularly intended for family entertainment.

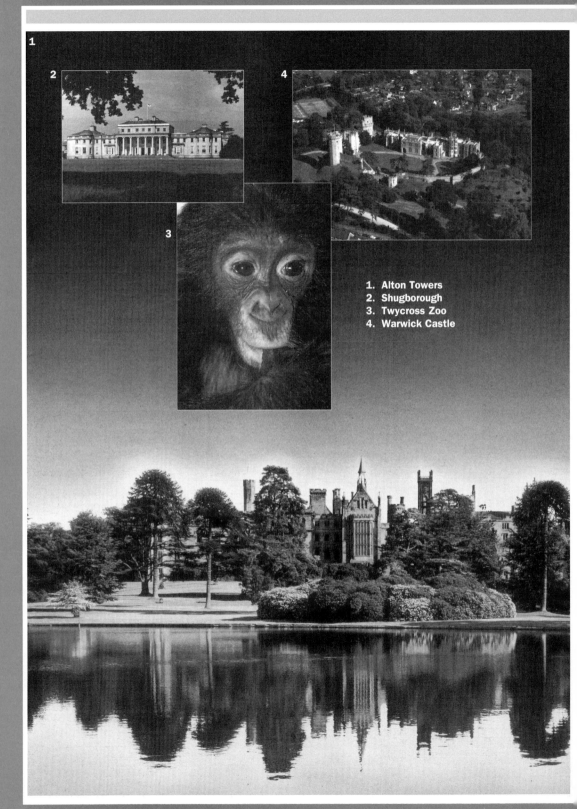

1. **Alton Towers**
2. **Shugborough**
3. **Twycross Zoo**
4. **Warwick Castle**

Alton Towers

Alton, near Stoke on Trent, Staffordshire

Britain's largest and most popular theme park is now so big that it offers a special price two day ticket because "there's too much to see in one day". The latest children's attraction is The Land of Make Believe, opened in 1993 as part of Alton's Celebrate Children Year, a fantasy land with a Chocolate House, World of Ice Cream, Magic Theatre and Children's World indoor play area for under-6s. Children can also join the Alton Towers Fun Club allowing them free admission for a year. The theme park covers 200 acres of grounds and contains 125 different rides and attractions. Its famous white-knuckle rides include the Corkscrew, the Black Hole, the Grand Canyon Rapids Ride and Thunderlooper, Britain's largest single loop rollercoaster. All types of catering are also available on site.

Open daily from the end of March to early November.

☎ 0538 702200

Alton Towers, Britain's largest and most popular theme park

The Haunted House and Characters, a fantasy land

The Farm

Blackbrook Animal and Bird World

Winkhill, near Leek, Staffordshire

Blackbrook cares for rare breeds of farm animals. The breeding programme means that at the right times of the year there are baby animals on view and the complex includes a pets corner especially for children. There are also various exotic bird species as well as pheasants and waterfowl. There is a shop and a picnic area.

Open every day except Wednesdays from Easter to the end of September.

☎ 0538 308293

Blenheim Palace

Woodstock, Oxfordshire

The Palace's grounds include a number of attractions for children including an adventure playground, a nature trail and a butterfly house. A narrow-gauge railway runs through the grounds. The Palace is the home of the Duke of Marlborough and was designed by Vanbrugh. The State Rooms contain displays of fine furniture, paintings, tapestries and sculpture as well as a Winston Churchill exhibition. The 2,000 acres of surrounding parkland were landscaped by Capability Brown and make magnificent use of water features. There is a garden centre within the park. There are restaurants, cafeterias, picnic spots and a gift shop.

Open daily from mid March until the end of October.

☎ 0993 811325

Blists Hill Open Air Museum

Ironbridge, Shropshire

All of the museums in the Ironbridge Gorge Museum complex have attractions for the family but Blists Hill is also the setting for special events throughout the year. These include May Pole dancing, sports evenings, Punch and Judy shows and a Bonfire Night Party. The museum staff have produced a leaflet with suggested touring routes around the complex including one to entertain the whole family and another specifically for families with young children. Ironbridge is the birthplace of the Industrial Revolution and Blists Hill recreates a Victorian working town at the height of the British Empire. All the locations in the museum are authentically restored, stocked with period goods and staff by workers in the appropriate dress of the era. The locations include the only working wrought ironworks in the developed world, two blast furnaces, a saw mill, printing shop, toll house, sweet shop, chemist's shop, bakers, pub, bank, church and squatter's cottage. There are shops, cafes and restaurants throughout the area.

Open all year except Christmas Eve and Christmas Day.

☎ 0952 433522

Bourton Model Village

Bourton-on-the-Water, Gloucestershire

Children [and adults] find it fascinating to wander amongst a world in miniature and imagine that the buildings are full size and they are giants and Bourton Model Village is one of the finest. Created in 1937 from Cotswold stone in the gardens of The Old New Inn, a village public house and hotel, it is a 1/9th scale model of the entire village of Bourton-on-the-Water as it appeared in the 1930s.

Closed on Christmas Day.

☎ 0451 20467

Broadway Tower Country Park

Broadway, Worcestershire

The park has a special children's pets area and one section of the grounds is reserved for ball games. Centred on Broadway's famous folly it includes nature walks through countryside full of wildlife, displays of rare breeds of animals and birds and an adventure playground. Refreshments are available and there are picnic areas in the Park.

Open daily from April to the end of October.

☎ 0386 852390

Children's Farm

Middleton, near Tamworth, Staffordshire

Devoted to introducing children to the joys of farming and animal husbandry. There are friendly farm animals, rare breeds and shire horses. The farm has play areas and picnic barns and can organise special events for birthdays.

Open all year.

☎ No telephone number.

Cotswold Farm Park Rare Breeds Centre

Guiting Power, near Bourton-on-the-Water, Gloucestershire

During the Summer there are special demonstrations on country crafts and farm skills as diverse as sheep shearing, bee keeping and wheelwrighting. The Centre houses the largest collection of rare farm breeds in Britain, it also features a farm trail, adventure playground, pets corner, shop and cafe.

Open April to September.

☎ 0451 850307

Cotswold Wildlife Park
Near Burford, Oxfordshire

Cotswold Wildlife Park hosts sponsored walks during the year and gives special demonstrations during the Summer. Amongst the most popular of these are the Snake Days when children have snakes explained to them and are encouraged to handle them. The park spreads over 120 acres and includes wildlife from across the world including white rhinos, tigers and leopards. There is also a butterfly house, a reptile house and an aquarium and the grounds also include picnic areas, a narrow-gauge railway, a brass-rubbing centre and an adventure playground.

Closed on Christmas Day

☎ 0993 823006

Cotswold Teddy Bear Museum
Broadway, Worcestershire

A must for children of all ages, this is one of the largest collections of teddy bears in the country. There are also displays of old dolls and toys and there is a shop.

Open every day.

☎ No telephone number.

Domestic Fowl Trust
Honeybourne, near Evesham, Worcestershire

The Trust runs a children's farm as part of its operation and children are encouraged to look after the baby chicks and handle them, there is also an adventure playground. The Trust is the home of a unique collection of 150 different breeds of turkey, geese, ducks and chickens. There is a tea room and a gift shop.

Open all year round except Fridays.

☎ 0386 833083

Drayton Manor Park and Zoo
Near Tamworth, Staffordshire

There are more than 50 rides and attractions for the whole family in this theme park. The leisure complex spreads over 160 acres and also includes a zoo and zoo farm, a garden centre, shops and restaurants.

Open every day from Easter to October.

☎ 0827 287979

Dudley Zoo and Castle
Dudley, West Midlands

Dudley Zoo and Castle organises special events around each school and public holiday and these include Punch and Judy Shows, donkey rides and face painting. The complex is centred around the ruins of Dudley Castle and includes an amusement park and and a children's adventure playground. The Zoo spreads over 40 acres of gardens and woodlands and holds approximately 1,000 animals in well-planned environments. There is a cafeteria.

Open except for Christmas Day.

☎ 0384 252401

Dudley Zoo

Fletchers Country Garden Centre
Eccleshall, Staffordshire

This extensive garden centre with show gardens has recently opened a new children's play area and also has a pets corner and a model steam railway. There is a craft centre where goods are made and sold. The complex includes an 18-hole continental crazy golf course and licensed tea rooms.

Open every day except Christmas and Boxing Day.

☎ 0785 851067

Folly Farm Waterfowl
Bourton-on-the-Water, Gloucestershire

A conservation centre for more than 160 species of wildfowl and waterfowl created on a 50 acre Cotswold farm with lakes and other natural environments. There are also farm animals and an undercover pets area.

Open all year.

☎ 0451 20285

Hartshill Hayes Country Park
Near Nuneaton, Warwickshire

136 acres of woodlands and hillside overlooking the Anker Valley. There are waymarked paths through the woods, picnic sites and a children's adventure playground. The site is reputedly where Queen Boudicca was defeated by the Romans.

Open all year.

☎ 0827 872660

Hatton Country World
Hatton, near Warwick, Warwickshire

Hatton Country World organises special events for families and children throughout the year. these range from demonstrations on sheep shearing, candle making and spinning and weaving to quad bike days, face painting and folk dancing. The three weekends before Christmas Day are special Father Christmas weekends. Hatton is the largest craft centre in the country and also houses a 100 acre farm with more than 40 rare breeds, a children's farm featuring Penny's Paddock which is presided over by Penny the Goat and a pets corner. There is a nature trail to the Grand Union Canal and an adventure playground.

Open all year except for the farm which is open daily between Easter and Christmas.

☎ 0926 843411

Himley Model Village
Himley Park, near Dudley, West Midlands

Children love exploring worlds in miniature and at Himley there is a collection of more than 80 model buildings including Dudley Market Place as it looked in the mid 1800s, Himley Hall, Himley Parish Church and the fictious village of the Archers, Ambridge. There is also a model yacht marina, a model Victorian tramway, a model railway and a working narrow-gauge railway which visitors can ride on.

Open daily between Easter and the end of October.

☎ 0902 895446

Jubilee Park
Symonds Yat West, Herefordshire

The Jubilee Park complex overlooks a beautiful stretch of the River Wye. One feature of the complex is an interactive fun museum especially designed for the young and young at heart. As with much of Jubilee Park the theme of the fun museum is mazes, there are games to play, mazes to solve and children can create mazes and see if the robot can solve them. Jubilee Park's other attractions include a famous hedge maze and the world's only museum of mazes. There is also a free-flying butterfly house as well as craft shops, a garden centre, riverside walks and a range of refreshments.

Open all year except for January when only the craft shops and garden centre open.

☎ 0600 890360

Moorlands Farm Park of British Rare Breeds
Near Stoke on Trent, Staffordshire

More than 70 rare breeds of cattle, sheep and pigs are cared for at Moorlands. Children are encouraged to get close to and feed the animals. There is also a pets corner and a children's play area. There is a shop where light refreshments are available in addition to a picnic area.

Open every day April to November.

☎ 0538 266479

Nature in Art - The International Centre for Wildlife Art
Twigworth, Gloucestershire

Nature in Art is currently building an Education Centre and when it is complete in Autumn 1993 it will become the home of a children's club dedicated to introducing youngsters to the enoyment and painting of nature. Nature in Art is a unique collection of wildlife art in all media housed in a Georgian mansion dating from 1740. The collection contains representative work from across the world ranging from traditional wildlife scenes to modern abstracts. The Centre also has artists in residence and, after the Education Centre opens, they will demonstrate to children methods of drawings, painting and sculpture. There is already a play area for children and new nature trails and special events are being organised. There is a coffee shop.

Closed over Christmas and Mondays except Bank Holidays.

☎ 0452 731422

Ryton Gardens National Centre for Organic Gardening
Ryton-on-Dunsmore, near Coventry, Warwickshire

Children are shown how gardens can be created and cultivated naturally using no pesticides or artificial fertilizers. Within the show gardens there are trees, shrubs, flowers, fruits, vegetables and herbs all being grown the natural way. The grounds include a lake, play area and a picnic site.

Open every day.

☎ 0203 303517

St. Augustine's Farm
Arlingham, Gloucestershire

Family groups and play groups are encouraged to visit this 124 acre working farm set around a bend in the River Severn. There is a wide range of farm animals including cows, goats, sheep, pigs and chicken and visitors are encouraged to feed the animals and bottle feed the newly born lambs. There is milking every day at 4 p.m. You can watch the farm at work, tour it on a tractor and trailer ride or walk the farm trail. There is also a display of early agricultural equipment, a children's play area and a tea and gift shop.

Only open during the summer unless by prior appointment

☎ 0452 740277

Severn Valley Railway
Bridgnorth, Shropshire

The Severn Valley Railway organises family and children's weekends throughout the year including Santa Specials during December and Thomas the Tank Engine weekends during the Summer school holidays. There is also a special Junior Club for children to join. The railway runs for 16 miles from Bridgnorth to Kidderminster and there are 6 stations along the line. Bridgnorth Station houses the UK's largest collection of standard gauge steam and diesel engines. The railway is in steam every weekend during the Summer and other facilities at Bridgnorth include a railway gift shop and a range of refreshments.

Station open all year, steam days every Saturday and Sunday from mid-May to early October, every Bank Holiday during the Summer and in December for the Santa Specials.

☎ 0299 403816

Shugborough Estate
Milford, near Stafford, Staffordshire

Shugborough organises special events on most weekends between April and December and many of these are designed to appeal to families and children. There are sheep shearing weekends, donkey days, doll and teddy bear fairs, goose fairs, sheep dog displays, craft festivals, a spectacular Bonfire Night party and Christmas carol singing. Shugborough Hall is an 18th century mansion set in a 900 acre estate and is the home of the Earl of Lichfield. The Hall's formal gardens include Victorian terraces and rose gardens. The surrounding parkland contains eight famous neo-Classical monuments and follies. There are extensive woodland walks through the estate. The estate's Home Farm is being used as a working 19th century farm with rare breeds and a restored corn mill. There is a special area of

the farm devoted to introducing children to farm animals. The estate also includes the Staffordshire County Museum. There are tea rooms, a shop and picnic areas.

Open every day between the end of March and the End of October.

☎ 0889 881388

Stratford-upon-Avon Shire Horse Centre
Near Stratford-upon-Avon, Warwickshire

The Centre organises special tours for children from toddlers to teenagers. It also has a pets corner where children are encouraged to hold and stroke small, friendly pets such as rabbits and guinea pigs. In season there are lambs and goat kids to watch. The shire horses at the Centre perform day-to-day work on the farm. There are many rare breeds of farm animals to see as well as riverside walks, an adventure playground, tea gardens and a shop.

Open all year.

☎ 0789 266276

Studley Castle Gardens
Winchcombe, Gloucestershire

The castle's children's adventure playground features a full size fort and a swing bridge as well as the normal range of climbing frames and swings. Studley Castle is a magnificent Tudor castle surrounded by splendid formal Elizabethan gardens. The castle hosts many craft events where local craftsmen demonstrate their skills. It also hosts a series of special events each year and has a plant centre selling examples of some of the castle's award winning roses. There is a restaurant as well as a gift shop.

Open from April to October.

☎ 0242 602308

Trentham Gardens

Trentham, Stoke on Trent,
Staffordshire

Trentham Gardens' attractions for children include a fun fair, go-karts and electric kiddie cars as well as an adventure playground. There are 800 acres of landscaped gardens, parkland and a lake. Watersports are available on the lake as is fly fishing. There is also a clay pigeon shooting facility. The gardens also have a nature reserve and deer park, mining and printing museums and a crafts centre. There is a restaurant and a cafe.

Open every day between Easter and October.

☎ 0782 657341

Trentham Gardens attractions include fun fair, go-karts and electric kiddie cars

Twycross Zoo
Near Twycross, Warwickshire

Twycross organises special events throughout the Summer.The zoo's education department runs the ZIP Squad [Zoo Interpretation Programme] to explain the working of the zoo to people of all ages. Pets Corner is the home of rabbits, guinea pigs and Vietnamese pot-bellied pigs and youngsters can often see some of the zoo's newest babies being cared for in this area. Twycross houses the finest collection of monkeys and other primates in the country. It is also the home of examples of many of the world's endangered species and has an impressive reptile house. There is a children's adventure playground and a self-service restaurant.

Open all year except Christmas Day.

☎ 0827 880250

Umberslade Children's Farm
Tanworth-in-Arden, near Solihull, Warwickshire

Umberslade has been developed to show children what life is like on a real farm. They can see the daily work of the farm and observe all of the wide variety of animals on the farm. There is also a children's playground. The farm shop sells a wide range of the farm's products including goat's milk and cheese and there is a picnic area.

Open daily from the end of March to the end of October.

☎ 05644 2251

Warwick Castle
Warwick, Warwickshire

Warwick Castle hosts a wide range of family entertainments on weekends between April and September including medieval days with jousting, firework displays and concerts. The castle is surrounded by 60 acres of grounds. There are exhibitions in the Great Hall, State Rooms, Armoury, Dungeons, Torture Chamber and Guy's Tower [named after Guy Beauchamp who was also called "The Black Dog of Arden"]. There are reconstructions using Madame Tussaud's waxworks, particularly the tableaux: "A Royal Weekend Party - 1898". The gardens around the castle include a Peacock Garden, Rose Gardens and a Conservatory. The rest of the grounds include woodlands and feature nature trails, riverside walks and woodland walks. There is a restaurant, catering and picnic areas. Warwick Castle is the most visited stately home in Britain.

Open every day except Christmas Day.

☎ 0926 495421

Warwick Doll Museum
Warwick, Warwickshire

A must for people of all ages this is one of the finest doll collections in the country. Housed in a building constructed around 1550 it has a unique collection of antique dolls and doll's houses. The exhibits also include toys, books, automata and prams.

Open daily between Easter and the end of September and during School Holidays.

☎ 0926 495546

West Midlands Safari and Leisure Park
Near Bewdley, Worcestershire

There are many children's activities in the Park including an amusement area with rides and attractions such as the Apple Rollercoaster and the Pirate Ship. A train carries visitors between the amusement area and the animal reserves. The reserves allow visitors to see the animals in their natural environments. The site also contains a reptile house, a sealion reserve with regular shows and a pets corner.

Open daily between April and October.

☎ 0299 402114

Weston Park
Near Shifnal, Shropshire

Weston Park holds family events throughout the Summer including Spring Fairs and Country Fayres. One particular favourite with children is the annual Pony Club Championship Trials in August. The grounds include a woodland adventure playground and a pets corner. The parklands were designed by Capability Brown and include a deer park containing a herd of fallow deer and flocks of rare breeds of sheep. Attractions in the grounds include a miniature railway, a tropical house, a museum and woodland walks. The house was built in early Restoration style in 1671. It contains impressive collections of furniture and tapestries and is particularly famous for its collection of fine art. There is a bar, a tea room and picnic areas.

Open daily in August, every day except Mondays and Fridays in June and July and all weekends and Bank Holidays between Easter and the end of September.

☎ 095 276 207

Wildfowl and Wetlands Trust
Slimbridge, Gloucestershire

Slimbridge hosts special themed weekends once a month and a Waterlands Festival in August with special puzzles and quizzes for children. One of the most popular times of the year with children is when the baby ducklings hatch. Slimbridge was founded in 1946 as the first of Sir Peter Scott's trusts and is the largest wildfowl collection in the world. The resident collection is around 3,300 birds from 164 species including around 400 flamingos. This collection is housed in 94 acres of ground and there are a further 800 acres as a temporary refuge for flocks of migrating wildfowl. There are many paths with hides, a gift shop and cafe.

Closed Christmas Eve and Christmas Day.

☎ 0453 890065

What's where and when

ALPHABETICAL LISTING OF ATTRACTIONS

A comprehensive listing of the attractions that can be found in the What to see... section [pages 32 to 71]. Each attraction's name is followed by a list of the classifications under which it appears in What to see... and detailed information can be found by looking up these main listings.

A

Abbey Dore Gardens - garden
Addersbury Lakes - wildlife
Acton Scott Historic Working Farm - food and drink
Aerospace Museum - museum
Alton Towers - the region at play
Amerton Working Farm - food and drink
Ancient High House - historic building
Annard Woollen Mill - working attraction
Anne Hathaway's Cottage - historic building
Arbury Hall - historic building
Ashleworth Tithe Barn - historic building
Aston Hall - historic building
Attingham Park - garden/historic building
Avoncroft Museum of Building - museum

B

Baddesley Clinton - historic building
Barnsley House Gardens - garden
Bass Museum - museum
Batsford Park - garden/wildlife
Berkeley Castle - garden/historic building
Berkeley Power Station - working attraction
Biddulph Grange Gardens - garden
Birdland - wildlife
Birmingham Botanical Gardens - garden
Birmingham Cathedral - religious building
Birmingham Railway Museum - steam railways
Birtsmorton Waterfowl Sanctuary - wildlife
Blackbrook Animal and Bird World - wildlife
Black Country Museum - museum
Blenheim Palace - garden/historic building/the region at play
Blists Hill Open Air Museum - museum
Bodlean Library - historic building
Bourton Model Village - the region at play
Brindley Mill - working attraction
Broadway Tower Country Park - the region at play
Brooklyn Farm - food and drink/working attraction
Broughton Castle - historic building
Burford House Gardens - garden
Burton Court - historic building
Buscot Park - garden/historic building

C

Cadbury World - food and drink
Charlecote Park - garden/historic building
Chatterley Whitfield Mining Museum - museum
Cheddleton Railway Centre - steam railways
Chedworth Roman Villa - antiquity

Chester House - historic building
Children's Farm - food and drink
Cider Museum - food and drink/museum
Coalbrookdale Furnace - museum
Coalport China Museum - museum
Coalport Minerva Works - working attraction
Conderton Pottery - working attraction
Coombe Abbey Country Park - wildlife
Cotswold Farm Park - the region at play/wildlife
Cotswold Motor Museum - museum
Cotswold Perfumery - working attraction
Cotswold Teddy Bear Museum - museum
Cotswold Water Park - the region at play
Cotswold Wildlife Park - the region at play/wildlife
Cotswold Woollen Weavers - working attractions
Coughton Court - historic building
Coventry Cathedral - religious building
Croft Castle - garden/historic building

D

Dean Forest Railway - steam railways
Didcot Railway Centre - steam railways
Domestic Fowl Trust - wildlife
Drayton Manor Park and Zoo - the region at play/wildlife
Dudley Zoo - the region at play/wildlife

E

Edinburgh Crystal - working attractions
Elgar's Birthplace - museum

F

Falconry Centre - wildlife
Fletchers Country Garden Centre - the region at play
Folly Farm Waterfowl - wildlife
Foxfield Steam Railway - steam railway
Frampton Court - garden/historic building

G

Gladstone Pottery Museum - museum
Glassbarn - working attraction
Gloucester Docks - the region at play
Goodrich Castle - historic building
Gloucester and Warwickshire Steam Railway - steam railway
Gloucester Cathedral - religious building

H

Hagley Hall - historic building
Hailes Abbey - religious building
Hall's Croft - historic building
Hanbury Hall - historic building
Hanch Hall - historic building
Hartshill Hayes Country Park - garden
Hatton Country World - the region at play
Hellens - historic buildings
Hereford Cathedral - religious building
Hidcote Manor Gardens - garden
Himley Model Village - the region at play
Hodnet Hall Gardens - garden

Holst's Birthplace - museum
Holy Trinity Church - religious building
Hoo Farm Country Park - food and drink
Hop Pocket Hop Farm - food and drink
House of the Tailor of Gloucester - the region at play
HP Bulmer Drinks - food and drink

I

Ironbridge Gorge Museum - museum
Izaac Walton Cottage Museum - museum

J

Jackfield Tile Museum - museum
James Gilbert Rugby Football Museum - museum
Jenner Museum - museum
Jinney Ring Craft Centre - working attraction
Jubilee Park - the region at play

K

Keith Harding's World of Mechanical Music - the region at play
Kelmscott Manor - historic building
Kenilworth Castle - historic building
Kingsbury Water Park - the region at play

L

Lichfield Cathedral - religious building
Lingen Nursery - garden
Little Malvern Court - historic building
Lord Leycester Hospital - historic building
Lost Street Museum - museum
Lower Brockhampton - historic building
Lunt Roman Fort - antiquity

M

Mary Arden's House - historic building
Mere, The - the region at play/wildlife
Midland Air Museum - museum
Moorlands Farm Park - wildlife
Moseley Hall - garden/historic building
Museum of British Road Transport - museum

N

National Birds of Prey Centre - wildlife
National Motorcycle Museum - museum
National Waterways Museum - museum
Nature in Art - museum
New Place - historic building

O

Oxford University Botanic Gardens - garden

P

Packwood House - garden/historic building
Pittville Pump Room - historic building

Prinknash Abbey Pottery - working attraction
Prinknash Bird Park - wildlife

Q

Queenswood Country Park - garden

R

Ragley Hall - garden/historic building/the region at play
Robert Opie Collection - museum
Royal Brierley Crystal - working attraction
Royal Doulton China - working attraction
Royal Doulton Crystal - working attraction
Royal Grafton China - working attraction
Royal Worcester China - working attraction
Ryton Gardens - garden

S

St. Augustine's Farm - food and drink
St. Chad's Cathedral - religious building
Sandwell Park Farm - food and drink
Severn Valley Railway - steam railway
Shakespeare's Birthplace - historic building
Sheldonian Theatre - historic building
Shrewsbury Abbey - religious building
Shrewsbury Castle - historic building
Shugborough - food and drink/garden/historic building
Snowshill Manor - historic building
Spode Works - working attraction
Stafford Castle - historic building
Stokesay Castle - historic building
Stratford Brass Rubbing Centre - the region at play
Stratford-upon-Avon Butterfly Farm - wildlife
Stratford-upon-Avon Shire Horse Centre - wildlife
Studley Castle - garden/historic building/the region at play

T

Tamworth Castle - historic building
Tewkesbury Abbey - religious building
Three Choirs Vineyard - food and drink
Tintern Abbey - religious building
Trentham Gardens - garden/the region at play
Tutbury Castle - historic building
Twycross Zoo - wildlife
Twyford Country Centre - the region at play

U

Umberslade Children's Farm - food and drink/wildlife
Upton House - historic building

W

Warwick Castle - garden/historic building/the region at play
Warwick Doll Museum - museum
Wedgwood Visitor Centre - working attraction
Westbury Court gardens - garden
West Midlands Safari and Leisure Park - the region at play/wildlife
Westonbirt Arboretum - garden

Weston Park - garden/historic building/the region at play
Wightwick Manor - historic building
Wilderhope Manor - historic building
Wildfowl and Wetlands Trust - wildlife
Winchcombe Pottery - working attraction
Worcester Cathedral - religious building
World of Butterflies - wildlife
Wroxeter Roman City - antiquity

ATTRACTIONS LISTED BY COUNTY

Gloucestershire

Ashleworth Tithe Barn - near Gloucester
Barnsley House Gardens - near Bibury
Batsford Park - near Moreton-in-the-Marsh
Berkeley Castle - Berkeley
Berkeley Power Station - Berkeley
Birdland - Bourton-on-the-Water
Bourton Model Village - Bourton-on-the-Water
Chedworth Roman Villa - near Cheltenham
Conderton Pottery - near Tewkesbury
Cotswold Farm Park - near Bourton-on-the-Water
Cotswold Motor Museum - Bourton-on-the-Water
Cotswold Perfumery - Bourton-on-the-Water
Cotswold Water Park - near Cirencester
Cotswold Woollen Weavers - near Lechlade
Dean Forest Railway - near Lydney
Folly Farm Waterfowl - Bourton-on-the-Water
Frampton Court - Frampton-upon-Severn
Glassbarn - Newent
Gloucester and Warwickshire Steam Railway - near Cheltenham
Gloucester Cathedral - Gloucester
Gloucester Docks - Gloucester
Hailes Abbey - near Winchcome
Hidcote Manor Gardens - near Chipping Campden
Holst's Birthplace - Cheltenham
House of the Tailor of Gloucester - Gloucester
Jenner Museum - Berkeley
Keith Harding's World of Mechanical Music - Northleach
National Birds of Prey Centre - Newent
National Waterways Museum - Gloucester
Nature in Art - Twigworth
Pittville Pump Room - Cheltenham
Prinknash Abbey Pottery - Painswick
Prinknash Bird Park - near Painswick
Robert Opie Collection - Gloucester
St. Augustine's Farm - Arlingham
Snowshill Manor - near Broadway
Studley Castle - Winchcombe
Tewkesbury Abbey - Tewkesbury
Three Choirs Vineyard - near Newent
Tintern Abbey - Tintern
Westbury Court Gardens - near Gloucester
Westonbirt Arboretum - near Tetbury
Wildfowl and Wetlands Trust - Slimbridge
Winchcombe Pottery - near Winchcombe

Herefordshire

Abbey Dore Gardens - near Pontrilas
Berrington Hall - near Leominster
Burton Court - near Leominster
Cider Museum - Hereford
Croft Castle - near Leominster
Goodrich Castle - near Ross-on-Wye
Hellens - Much Marcle
Hereford Cathedral - Hereford
Hop Pocket Hop Farm - near Bishops Frome
HP Bulmer Drinks - Hereford
Jubilee Park - Symonds Yat West
Lingen Nursery and Gardens - near Leominster
Lost Street Museum - Ross-on-Wye
Lower Brockhampton - near Bromyard
Queenswood Country Park - near Leominster
World of Butterflies - Symonds Yat West

Oxfordshire

Addersbury Lakes - near Bloxham
Blenheim Palace - Woodstock
Bodlean Library - Oxford
Broughton Castle - near Banbury
Buscot Park - Faringdon
Cotswold Wildlife Park - near Burford
Didcot Railway Centre - Didcot
Kelmscott Manor - near Faringdon
Oxford University Botanical Gardens - Oxford
Sheldonian Theatre - Oxford
Upton House - near Banbury

Shropshire

Acton Scott Historic Working Farm - near Church Stretton
Attingham Park - near Shewsbury
Blists Hill Open Air Museum - Ironbridge
Coalbrookdale Furnace - Ironbridge
Coalport China Museum - Ironbridge
Hodnet Hall Gardens - near Market Drayton
Hoo Farm Country Park - near Telford
Ironbridge Gorge Museum - Ironbridge
Jackfield Tile Museum - Ironbridge
Mere, The - Ellesmere
Severn Valley Railway - Bridgnorth
Shrewsbury Abbey - Shrewsbury
Shrewsbury Castle - Shrewsbury
Stokesay Casle - Craven Arms
Weston Park - near Shifnal
Wilderhope Manor - near Much Wenlock
Wroxeter Roman City - near Shewsbury

Staffordshire

Alton Towers - near Stoke on Trent
Amerton Working Farm - near Stafford

Ancient High House - Stafford
Bass Museum - Burton-upon-Trent
Biddulph Grange Gardens - Biddulph
Blackbrook Animal and Bird World - near Leek
Brindley Mill - Leek
Brooklyn Farm and Craft Workshop - near Stoke on Trent
Chatterley Whitfield Mining Museum - near Stoke on Trent
Cheddleton Railway Centre - near Leek
Children's Farm - near Tamworth
Coalport Minerva Works - Stoke on Trent
Drayton Manor - near Tamworth
Fletchers Country Garden Centre - Eccleshall
Foxfield Steam Railway - Stoke on Trent
Gladstone Pottery Museum - Stoke on Trent
Hanch Hall - Lichfield
Izaak Walton Cottage Museum - near Stone
Lichfield Cathedral - Lichfield
Moorlands Farm Park - near Stoke on Trent
Royal Doulton China - Stoke on Trent
Royal Grafton China - Stoke on Trent
Shugborough - near Stafford
Spode Works - Stoke on Trent
Stafford Castle - near Stafford
Tamworth Castle - Tamworth
Trentham Gardens - Stoke on Trent
Tutbury Castle - Tutbury
Wedgwood Visitor Centre - near Stoke on Trent

Warwickshire

Anne Hathaway's Cottage - near Stratford-upon-Avon
Arbury Hall - near Nuneaton
Baddesley Clinton - near Knowle
Charlecote Park - near Warwick
Chester House - Knowle
Coughton Court - near Alcester
Hall's Croft - Stratford-upon-Avon
Hatton Country World - near Warwick
Hartshill Hayes Country Park - near Nuneaton
Holy Trinity Church - Stratford-upon-Avon
James Gilbert Rugby Football Museum - Rugby
Kenilworth Castle - Kenilworth
Kingsbury Water Park - near Tamworth
Lord Leycester Hospital - Warwick
Mary Arden's House - near Stratford-upon-Avon
New Place - Stratford-upon-Avon
Packwood House - near Lapworth
Ragley Hall - near Alcester
Shakespeare's Birthplace - Stratford-upon-Avon
Stratford Brass Rubbing Centre - Stratford-upon-Avon
Stratford-upon-Avon Butterfly Farm - Stratford-upon-Avon
Stratford-upon-Avon Shire Horse Centre - near Stratford-upon-Avon
Twycross Zoo - near Twycross
Umberslade Children's Farm - near Solihull
Warwick Castle - Warwick
Warwick Doll Museum - Warwick

West Midlands

Aston Hall - Birmingham
Birmingham Botanical Gardens - Birmingham

Birmingham Cathedral - Birmingham
Birmingham Railway Museum - Birmingham
Black Country Museum - Dudley
Cadbury World - Bournville
Coombe Abbey Country Park - near Coventry
Coventry Cathedral - Coventry
Dudley Zoo - Dudley
Edinburgh Crystal - Stourbridge
Himley Model Village - near Dudley
Lunt Roman Fort - near Coventry
Midland Air Museum - near Coventry
Moseley Hall - near Wolverhampton
Museum of British Road Transport - Coventry
National Motorcycle Museum - near Birmingham
Royal Brierley Crystal - Birmingham
Royal Doulton Crystal - Stourbridge
Ryton Gardens - near Coventry
St. Chad's Cathedral - Birmingham
Sandwell Park Farm - near West Bromwich
Wightwick Manor - near Wolverhampton

Worcestershire

Annard Woollen Mill - near Evesham
Avoncroft Museum of Buildings - near Bromsgrove
Birtsmorton Waterfowl Sanctuary - near Malvern
Broadway Tower Country Park - Broadway
Burford House Gardens - near Tenbury Wells
Cotswold Teddy Bear Museum - Broadway
Domestic Fowl Trust - near Evesham
Elgar's Birthplace - near Worcester
Falconry Centre - near Kidderminster
Hagley Hall - near Stourbridge
Hanbury Hall - near Droitwich Spa
Jinney Ring Craft Centre - near Bromsgrove
Little Malvern Court - Malvern
Royal Worcester China - Worcester
Twyford Country Centre - near Evesham
West Midlands Safari and Leisure Park - near Bewdley
Worcester Cathedral - Worcester

ATTRACTIONS IN OR NEAR TO THE HEART OF ENGLAND'S MAIN TOWNS

BIRMINGHAM

Aston Hall
Birmingham Botanical Gardens
Birmingham Cathedral
Birmingham Railway Museum
Black Country Museum
Cadbury World
Dudley Zoo
Himley Model Village
Moseley Hall
National Motorcycle Museum
Royal Brierley Crystal
Ryton Gardens
St. Chad's Cathedral
Sandwell Park Farm

BURTON-UPON-TRENT

Bass Museum

CHELTENHAM

Gloucester and Warwickshire Steam Railway
Holst's Birthplace
Pittville Pump Room

COVENTRY

Coombe Abbey Country Park
Coventry Cathedral
Lunt Roman Fort
Midland Air Museum
Museum of British Road Transport

GLOUCESTER

Ashleworth Tithe Barn
Gloucester Cathedral
Gloucester Docks
House of the Tailor of Gloucester
National Waterways Museum
Robert Opie Collection
Westbury Court

HEREFORD

Cider Museum
Hereford Cathedral
HP Bulmer Drinks

LICHFIELD

Hanch Hall
Lichfield Cathedral

OXFORD

Blenheim Palace
Bodlean Library
Didcot Railway Centre
Oxford University Botanic Gardens
Sheldonian Theatre

ROSS-ON-WYE

Goodrich Castle
Jubilee Park
Lost Street Museum

SHREWSBURY

Attingham Park
Shrewsbury Abbey
Shrewsbury Castle
Wroxeter Roman City

STAFFORD

Ancient High House
Shugborough
Stafford Castle

STOKE ON TRENT

Alton Towers
Brooklyn Farm and Craft Workshop
Chatterley Whitfield Mining Museum
Coalport Minerva Works
Foxfield Steam Railway
Gladstone Pottery Museum
Moorlands Farm Park
Royal Doulton China
Royal Grafton China
Spode Works
Trentham Gardens
Wedgwood Visitor Centre

STRATFORD-UPON-AVON

Anne Hathaway's Cottage
Hall's Croft
Holy Trinity Church
Mary Arden's House
New Place
Shakespeare's Birthplace
Stratford Brass Rubbing Centre
Stratford-upon-Avon Butterfly Farm
Stratford-upon-Avon Shire Horse Centre

TELFORD

Blists Hill Open Air Museum
Coalbrookdale Furnace
Coalport China Museum
Ironbridge Gorge Museum
Jackfield Tile Museum

WARWICK

Charlecote Park
Hatton Country World
Kenilworth Castle
Lord Leycester Hospital
Warwick Castle
Warwick Doll Museum

WORCESTER

Elgar's Birthplace
Royal Worcester China
Worcester Cathedral

ALWAYS OPEN

The following attractions are open at least six days a week throughout the year.
Each attraction's name is followed by a list of the classifications under which it appears in the What to See... section [pages 32 to 71]. The attraction's main listing under these classifications will provide information on which day, if any, the attraction closes. Please note that the vast majority of attractions have limited opening over the Christmas period.

A

Addersbury Lakes - wildlife
Aerospace Museum - museum
Amerton Working Farm - food and drink
Ancient High House - historic building
Annard Woollen Mill - working attraction
Anne Hathaway's Cottage - historic building
Attingham Park - garden

B

Bass Museum - museum
Birdland - wildlife
Birmingham Botanical Gardens - garden
Birmingham Cathedral - religious building
Birmingham Railway Museum - steam railways
Birtsmorton Waterfowl Sanctuary - wildlife
Blists Hill Open Air Museum - museum
Bourton Model Village - the region at play
Burford House Gardens - garden

C

Cadbury World - food and drink
Chatterley Whitfield Mining Museum - museum
Children's Farm - food and drink
Cider Museum - museum
Coalbrookdale Furnace - museum
Coalport China Museum - museum
Conderton Pottery - working attraction

Coombe Abbey Country Park - wildlife
Cotswold Perfumery - working attraction
Cotswold Teddy Bear Museum - museum
Cotswold Water Park - the region at play
Cotswold Wildlife Park - the region at play/wildlife
Coventry Cathedral - religious building
Croft Castle - garden

D

Dean Forest Railway - steam railway
Didcot Railway Centre - steam railways
Domestic Fowl Trust - wildlife
Dudley Zoo - the region at play/wildlife

E

Edinburgh Crystal - working attraction

F

Falconry Centre - wildlife
Fletchers Country Garden Centre - the region at play
Folly Farm Waterfowl - wildlife
Frampton Court - garden/historic building

G

Gloucester and Warwickshire Steam Railway - steam railways
Gloucester Cathedral - religious building
Gloucester Docks - the region at play
Goodrich Castle - historic building

H

Hall's Croft - historic building
Hartshill Hayes Country Park - garden
Hatton Country World - the region at play
Hereford Cathedral - religious building
Holy Trinity Church - religious building
House of the Tailor of Gloucester - the region at play

I

Ironbridge Gorge Museum - museum

J

Jackfield Tile Museum - museum
James Gilbey Rugby Football Museum - museum
Jinney Ring Craft Centre - working attraction

K

Kelmscott Manor - historic building
Keith Harding's World of Mechanical Music - the region at play
Kingsbury Water Park - the region at play

L

Lichfield Cathedral - religious building
Lord Leycester Hospital - historic building

M

Mary Arden's House - historic building
Mere, The - wildlife
Museum of British Road Transport - museum

N

National Motorcycle Museum - museum
National Waterways Museum - museum
Nature in Art - museum
New Place - historic building

O

Oxford University Botanic Gardens - garden

P

Prinknash Abbey Pottery - working attraction
Prinknash Bird park - wildlife

Q

Queenswood Country Park - garden

R

Robert Opie Collection - museum
Royal Worcester China - working attraction
Ryton Gardens - garden

S

St. Chad's Cathedral - religious building
Sanswell Park Farm - food and drink
Severn Valley Railway - steam railway
Shakespeare's Birthplace - historic building
Shrewsbury Castle - historic building
Shrewsbury Cathedral - religious building
Stafford Castle - historic building
Stratford-upon-Avon Butterfly Farm - wildlife
Stratford-upon-Avon Shire Horse Centre - wildlife

T

Tamworth Castle - historic building
Tewkesbury Abbey - religious building
Tintern Abbey - religious building
Twycross Zoo - wildlife
Twyford Country Centre - the region at play

W

Warwick Castle - garden/historic building/the region at play
Wedgwood Visitor Centre - working attraction
Westonbirt Arboretum - garden
Wildfowl and Wetlands trust - wildlife
Winchcombe Pottery - working attraction
Worcester Cathedral - religious building
Wroxeter Roman City - antiquity

WORTH VISITING BUT BEWARE

The following attractions are well worth visiting but are only open for limited periods.

Each attraction's name is followed by a list of the classifications under which it appears in the What to see... section [pages 32 to 71] and a guide to its opening. [S] means that the attraction is only open during the Summer months, normally from Easter to October. [R] means that the attraction has restricted opening, normally three days a week or less. To find out exactly when the attraction is open you should look up the main listings under the relevant classifications in What to see...

A

Abbey Dore Gardens - garden [S]
Acton Scott Historic Working Farm - food and drink [S]
Alton Towers - the region at play [S]
Arbury Hall - historic building [R], [S]
Ashleworth Tithe Barn - historic building [S]
Aston Hall - historic building [S]
Attingham Park - historic building [S]

B

Baddesley Clinton - historic building [S]
Berkeley Castle - garden/historic building [S]
Berrington Hall - historic building [S]
Biddulph Grange Gardens - garden [S]
Blackbrook Animal and Bird World - wildlife [S]
Blenheim Palace - garden/historic building/the region at play [S]
Brindley Mill - working attraction [S]
Broadway Tower Country Park - the region at play [S]
Broughton Castle - historic building[R], [S]
Burton Court - historic house [R], [S]
Buscot Park - garden/historic building [R], [S]

C

Charlecote Park - garden/historic building [S]
Cheddleton Railway Centre - steam railways [S]
Chedworth Roman Villa - antiquity [S]
Cotswold Farm Park - the region at play/wildlife [S]
Coughton Court - historic building [S]
Croft Castle - historic building [S]

D

Drayton Manor - the region at play/wildlife [S]

F

Foxfield Steam Railway - steam railway [R]

H

Hagley Hall - historic building [R]
Hanbury Hall - historic building [R], [S]
Hanch Hall - historic building [R], [S]
Hellens - historic building [R], [S]
Hidcote Manor Gardens - garden [S]

Himley Model Village - the region at play [S]
Hodnet Hall Gardens - garden [S]
Hoo Farm Country Park - food and drink [S]

J

Jenner Museum - museum [R]

L

Little Malvern Court - historic building [S]
Lower Brockhampton - historic building [S]
Lunt Roman Fort - antiquity [S]

M

Midland Air Museum - museum [S]
Moseley Hall - garden/historic building [S]

P

Packwood House - garden/historic building [S]

R

Ragley Hall - garden/historic building/the region at play [S]

S

St. Augustine's Farm - food and drink [S]
Shugborough - garden/historic building [S]
Stratford Brass Rubbing Centre - the region at play [S]
Studley Castle - garden/historic building/the region at play [S]

T

Trentham Gardens - garden/the region at play [S]
Tutbury Castle - historic building [S]

U

Umberslade Children's Farm - wildlife [S]

W

Warwick Doll Museum - museum [S]
Westbury Court Gardens - garden [S]
West Midlands Safari and Leisure Park - the region at play/wildlife [S]
Weston Park - historic building/the region at play [S]
Wightwick Manor - historic building [S]
Wilderhope Manor - historic building [R]